GLOBAL BIOETHICS
Building on the Leopold Legacy

by
Van Rensselaer Potter

Michigan State University Press
1988

Michigan State University Press
East Lansing, Michigan 48823-5202

Production: Julie L. Loehr
Editing: Ellen M. Link
Cover Design: Lynne A. Brown
Text Design: Coletta A. Perry
Typography: the Copyfitters, Ltd.
Printing: Edward Brothers, Inc.

Potter, Van Rensselaer, 1911–
    Global bioethics.

    Bibliography: p.
    Includes index.
    1. Bioethics.   2. Medical ethics.   I. Title.
QH332.P68   1988   179'.1   88-42901
ISBN 0-87013-264-4

This book is dedicated to Vivian,
our grandchildren,
Lisa,
Mabs,
Eleanora,
Joshua,
Jeremy,
and Jesse,
and all other grandchildren who
will inherit the 21st century.

CONTENTS

FOREWORD

IDEAS HAVE A LIFE AND POWER of their own. An idea can shape or reshape the ways in which we understand and experience reality. Encountering a fruitful idea, we say, Ah-ha! and see the world anew and cannot imagine it otherwise. The ideas that shape our vision of ourselves and our reality structure the very taken-for-granted character of everyday life. The same at times happens with new words. A new word often allows us to name elements of reality in a way that conveys new control over our cultural environment. It is often not the precision of a word that is the source of its power and usefulness. In fact, it is often the imprecision, the lack of clarity, that allows us to name and bring together at one time many areas of interest. An apt word can assemble a rich set of images and meanings and thus help us to see relations between elements of reality that were previously separated in our vision and thought of only as disparate. Such a word has a fertile or strategic ambiguity. This has been the case with "bioethics."

In the 1960s there was a growing concern to understand and master our rapidly developing sciences and technologies. The aspiration to value-free science was being recognized as not only vain but misleading. It was appreciated that science and technology don't just spring from a culture but influence and have their full meaning within a culture as well. But the sciences and technologies appeared severed from their ancient links with the humanities, from the traditional aspiration to understand all human powers within the concerns of central human goals and ambitions. Hence, the 1960s were marked in the history of science by a concerted effort to understand the development of the sciences within their cultural and historical context. The relation of the humanities to science and technology became, at least theoretically, more nuanced with the publication of books such as Thomas Kuhn's *The Structure of Scientific Revolutions.*

Within the technologies there was a beginning appreciation that education in the values that direct a technology should be integral to the training of a good technologist. Technologies and applied sciences, after all, are robustly goal-directed. They are shaped by non-epistemic goals, goals that have to do with the structuring or reshaping of reality and the costs involved in such undertakings. In a technology or applied science, one does not seek to know a thing truly for its own sake but because of its usefulness toward achieving other goals. This is particularly true in medicine. One investigates anatomy, physiology, bacteriology, immunology, and so forth within medicine, not primarily to know truly but to intervene effectively, in order to preserve or restore health and to alleviate pain, distress, and suffering. But concepts of health and disease, of pain and suffering, are subtly contoured by cultures and their understandings of human well-being.

Moreover, when applied sciences or technologies are as expensive and as intrusive as those of medicine, questions of proper procedures for individual and societal choice and authorization become central.

Such, in fact, has been recognized to be the case. By the close of the 1960s, there was an interest in understanding the values and images of human well-being that underlie the practices of medicine, nursing, and allied health sciences. There was already a realization that, in the future, we will be able to engage in genetic engineering and develop technologies with radically new implications. Thus, the focus was also on the basic biomedical sciences, which would or could in the end lead to developments that would change medicine and ourselves. The old terms—medical ethics or nursing ethics—appeared too narrow or parochial to identify this wide-ranging cluster of interests and concerns. Even the term "biomedical ethics" appeared too narrow. In the midst of all this, in 1971, as the first centers for bioethics were being formed, Van Rensselaer Potter published *Bioethics: Bridge to the Future.* The term brought together a wide range of interests. It was like a nidus dropped in a supersaturated solution. At once, a whole range of concerns crystallized. The word "bioethics" did brilliant service in bringing together a wide cluster of important cultural concerns. The term was profoundly heuristic.

But Professor Potter had intended to address an even broader range of issues. Using the term bioethics, he wanted to investigate concerns that focused on the issue of human survival. He hoped to bring attention to the ways in which science can help better formulate our understanding of humanity and the world. He suggested ways in which we could conduct ourselves more responsibly and better achieve a life of quality. Bioethics was proposed by Potter as a term for a discipline that could provide a science for survival and aid in securing happier and more productive lives. Potter's focus remains broader than that of most contemporary bioethicists. He offers a global perspective with an ecological focus on how we as humans will guide our adaptation to our environment.

Since the publication of his book, *Bioethics,* the term has developed its own history with little regard to Potter's original intentions. It is like a child who left home, renouncing the disciplines of its father but with substantial talents and capacities of its own. It has willfully chartered its own successful but narrower destiny by spawning an *Encyclopedia of Bioethics* and a large number of volumes and essays on bioethics, as well as a journal by that name. For the most part, the term bioethics has been taken to identify the disciplined analysis of the moral and conceptual assumptions of medicine, the biomedical sciences, and the allied health professions. As such, it has become a special area of philosophy or ethics, even though all of its practitioners have not been formally trained in either area. The field of bioethics has succeeded in identifying the need of the sciences and arts of health care for the humanities. The field has also given the humanities—philosophy and ethics in particular— an opportunity to discharge one of the traditional obligations of the liberal arts: to protect our freedom as persons by helping us to understand our condition and circumstances better. In all of this, the more general meaning of Potter's term has been overshadowed by the great success it has had in bringing issues together for examination in the area of health care.

In this volume Potter is reminding us once more of the more general promise of the term "bioethics." He is again recalling us to the concerns of his 1971 publication: we must reflect on the values ingredient in our relationship to nature if we are to secure our continued survival in a way that will accord with our views of our own well-being. In the future, we will be able explicitly to control the adaptation of our species to the world. Our expanding scientific and technological base allows us to change not only the character of our environment but the character of our human nature as well. We have been changing the character of the earth at least since the development of agriculture. We have altered ourselves through immunizations, which allow more children to grow to reproductive age and more people to live together in crowded cities. We have orchestrated our human nature through contraception and sterilization, which allow us willfully to direct our reproduction. In the future, however distant, adaptation will surely take place through our ever more fundamental and self-conscious shaping and reshaping of our human nature. Even the very modest short-term promises of genetic engineering suggest a long-term future in which we will make ourselves the objects of our own manipulations. The moral and public policy challenge now confronts us of understanding what we should do when and why, and who has the authority to decide.

Global Bioethics: Building on the Leopold Legacy provides us with a particular land ethic for one of the most important areas of public policy discussion. But more generally, Potter shows again why the term bioethics can usefully sustain his original broader intent. Within the compass of bioethics broadly construed, we will need to understand what kinds of values concerning the environment impose what kinds of obligations. Given the long history of species extinction, need we be concerned with the survival of all species or only some species, and if some, which? In attempting to protect the environment, we must choose among ways in which we can conceive of an ideal preservation of nature. Must we in the end preserve nature as one would develop and manicure a park? Is it possible at all to imagine maintaining any or many large tracts of land in their "natural" state, unaltered or untouched by man? Does one "maintain" indigenous humans living a traditional life as a part of the original ecological balance? To choose among these possibilities is to choose among different visions of man's relationship to nature and among different visions of the value and importance of nature. As Potter points out, such choices will themselves depend on particular population policies. In all of this, we will need to ask whether anyone or any government has the authority to select a particular vision or set of visions and impose it uniformly on the world. Here, questions concerning the character or limits of human individual and communal authority rise to challenge us. And if we can identify the proper goals to be pursued and have the authority to pursue them, are they best pursued under governmental or private auspices?

Potter makes a rich and important contribution to the kinds of discussions and explorations we will need to undertake. The scope of bioethics is as encompassing as he suspected in 1971 and larger than most have acknowledged. Whether or not one agrees with the particular vision Potter gives us, one will need to acknowledge that the genre of issues he addresses is inescapable. As with his original contribution of the term bioethics, he is again making a contribution that reaches beyond the particularity of his statement to a general philosophical and moral challenge that we will all need to confront.

—H. TRISTRAM ENGELHARDT, JR.
Center for Ethics, Medicine, and Public Issues
Houston, Texas

PREFACE

TODAY WE CAN no longer write about the ethics for human survival without reference to our intellectual ancestors. There is little doubt that Aldo Leopold was one of those ancestors. With his name cited in 27 of 96 articles in the first eighteen issues of the journal, *Environmental Ethics,* he strongly influenced the development of what we shall describe as ecological bioethics. His book, *A Sand County Almanac,* contains no bibliography, and the original paper entitled "The Conservation Ethic," published in *The Journal of Forestry,*[1] also contained no bibliography. When this essay was revised and enlarged for inclusion in the *Almanac* as "The Land Ethic," no references had been added. As the first person to couple and define the words "land" and "ethic" in ecological terms, Leopold was unquestionably the first bioethicist; he was first to envision a new ethical basis for human conduct, first to develop an ecological ethic (which he called the land ethic), and first to explain clearly why it is needed. In these respects, he had no need of, and no avenue of approach that acknowledged, a progenitor.

We who follow Aldo Leopold are obligated to note not only his pioneering efforts but also the publications of the new breed of concerned biologists, ecologists, and people of many disciplines who are concerned with the problem of acceptable survival for the human species. The issue, in plain English, is "What We Must Do," to use the title of a 1969 article by John Platt, published in *Science*.[2] Others who must be recognized in the development of ecological bioethics are Rachel Carson, Lewis Mumford, Eugene P. Odum, Garrett Hardin, Paul Ehrlich, Barry Commoner, Lester R. Brown, Richard Falk, and Paul Shepard.

But there are many others who cannot be cited in the present account. Fortunately, a 1985 book entitled *Deep Ecology*[3] (utilizing the phrase coined by Arne Naess in 1973), which traces the basic concepts back to Aldo Leopold, attempted to cite just about all the relevant views and to quote them at length. The authors define *deep ecology* as an attempt "to articulate a comprehensive religious and philosophical worldview" that "goes beyond a limited piecemeal shallow approach to environmental problems" (Devall and Sessions, 65). Thus, the phrase deep ecology can be understood as essentially synonymous with what I would call "bioethical ecology," but the present work insists that bioethical medicine is a necessary component of the deep ecology effort to "ask what kind of a society would be best for maintaining a particular ecosystem" (65). The myriad questions raised by modern medical technology are not discussed by the authors of *Deep Ecology,* but their effort is an excellent complement to the present effort to develop a global bioethic that deals with the medical dilemmas.

A recent annotated bibliography by Mary Angle-meyer and Eleanor R. Seagraves contains 857 entries that pertain to attitudes and values relevant to *The Natural Environment.*[4] They cannot all be cited in the pages to follow, but where a source is recognized it will be cited.

I am indebted to the University of Chicago Press for permission to reproduce most of my article from *Perspectives in Biology and Medicine* (Winter 1987) entitled "Two Kinds of Bioethics: Aldo Leopold's Land Ethic Revisited"; to the University of Wisconsin Press for permission to quote from *Aldo Leopold. His Life and Work* (1988) by Curt Meine, and to Curt Meine for providing me with helpful pages from his manuscript prior to its publication; to the Oxford University Press for permission to quote from *A Sand County Almanac Commemorative Edition* by Aldo Leopold and from *The Foundations of Bioethics* (1986) by H. Tristram Engelhardt, Jr.; to Rochelle N. Shain for permission to quote at length from sections of *Fertility Control,* which she edited with Carl J. Pauerstein; to the American Association for Cancer Research for permission to reproduce figure 3 from my article in *Cancer Research*[5] and to Nina Leopold Bradley and Charles Bradley for their invitation to participate in the 1987 Summer Seminar Series held outdoors in the dooryard of the Leopold "Shack," and to present a lecture on Leopold's Neglected Legacy, here reproduced in part in chapter 1.

Especially appreciated is the accurate typing of the manuscript by Mary Jo Markham, and the critical editing by Ellen Link of the Michigan State University Press. I also thank my daughter, Karin Potter Simon, and Professor James E. Trosko for helpful suggestions.

Aldo Leopold criticized academic professors and their specializations and commented, using a musical metaphor, that all scientists "are restrained by an ironbound taboo which decrees that the construction of instruments is the domain of science, while the detection of harmony is the domain of poets." There is much evidence that he preferred to advocate his intuitive ideas by means of poetic prose rather than by tables or charts. He had as much need for a bibliography as would a poem by T. S. Eliot or W. H. Auden, or a symphony by Mozart.[6] Fifty years later, we cannot rest the case on poetry alone; but I urge the reader to return to *A Sand County Almanac* and savor the romantic as well as the philosophic passages in that memorable volume.

---

1. Aldo Leopold, "The Conservation Ethic," *Journal of Forestry* 31 (1933): 634–43.
2. John Platt, "What We Must Do," *Science* 166 (1969): 1115–21.
3. Bill Devall and George Sessions, *Deep Ecology* (Salt Lake City: 4Peregrine Smith Books, 1985). Excellent coverage of past books and articles. Unfortunately lacks author or subject indexes.
4. Mary Anglemeyer and Eleanor R. Seagraves, *The Natural Environment, An Annotated Bibliography on Attitudes and Values* (Washington, D.C.: Smithsonian Institution Press, 1984).
5. Van Rensselaer Potter, "Humility with Responsibility—A Bioethic for Oncologists," Presidential Address, *Cancer Research* 35 (1975): 2297–2306.
6. Although Leopold formally acknowledged no antecedents in composing "The Land Ethic," I hasten to point out that in building his monumental textbook *Game Management* he drew on many sources. His book has tables, charts, photographs, an extensive glossary, an index, and a bibliography containing 427 citations by my count. It was the first book of its kind; it created a new profession.

INTRODUCTION

In 1971 A BASIC TENET OF BIOETHICS was that ethical values cannot be separated from biological facts.[1] At about the same time that my book *Bioethics, Bridge to the Future* appeared, bioethics as an outgrowth of medical ethics was being developed at Georgetown University and at the Hastings Institute. For many it came to mean exclusively the ethics of how far to exercise the medical options that are technically possible, such as organ transplants, the use of artificial organs, abortion, sterilization, artificial contraception, chemotherapy, informed consent by the patient, freedom of choice in procreation or abortion, fertilization *in vitro,* surrogate pregnancy, and future developments in genetic engineering. These issues in general have short-term, immediately visible consequences and all have to do with the maintenance and prolongation of individual lives. With the focus on medical options, the fact that bioethics had been proposed to combine human values with ecological facts was forgotten by

many: the ethics of how far to exercise technological options in the exploitation of the environment
was not associated with the term bioethics.

The time has come to recognize that we can no
longer examine medical options without considering ecological science and the larger problems of
society on a global scale. An example of an issue in
global bioethics involves the medical options concerning human fertility in confrontation with the
ecological need to limit the exponential increase in
the human population. Regardless of the advances
in health care—not to mention those in agricultural
production, conservation of natural resources, and
preservation of the natural environment—no program can hope to succeed without the acceptance
of controlled human fertility as a basic ethical
imperative for the human species. Yet any ethical
framework that accepts this premise will obviously
run counter to some of the ethical positions taken
by several of the most powerful religious and political groups that exist today.

When I coined the word "bioethics" in 1970, I
was influenced by C. H. Waddington perhaps more
than by any other individual. Born in 1905, he
served as professor of animal genetics in Edinburgh
from 1946, gaining expertise in embryology, genetics, and evolution. He became essentially a bioethicist before the word was invented, a man concerned
with the need to develop ethical theory in the light
of biological knowledge, an aim similar to my own.
"What is demanded of each generation is a theory
of ethics which is neither a mere rationalization of
prejudices, nor a philosophical discourse so abstract
as to be irrelevant to the practical problems with
which mankind is faced at that time."[2] He was aware
of the philosophers' claim that it is logically impossible to pass from "is" to "ought" and that to make
such an attempt is to commit the "naturalistic
fallacy." He said first,

> We can with perfect logical consistency, conceive of an aim or principle of policy which, while not in itself in its essence an ethical rule, would enable us to judge between different ethical rules. It is for such a principle that I am searching, and which I claim to be discoverable in the notion which I have referred to as 'biological wisdom.' . . . To a theory which attempted to discover a criterion for judging between ethical systems the refutation of the naturalistic fallacy would be largely beside the point. (50–59)

Earlier he had said,

> In the lifetime of any human individual these three types of activity—becoming an ethicizing being, formulating one particular system of ethical beliefs, and criticizing those beliefs by some supra-ethical criterion of wisdom—are not clearly separated in time but certainly overlap with one another.

Here he defined the supra-ethical criterion as "the general good," "the ethical system of general validity," or as "biological wisdom" (26–27). I insist that survival is an even more basic supra-ethical criterion.

I was also influenced by an article by Margaret Mead asserting, "We need in our universities . . . Chairs of the Future,"[3] which inspired me to assume the role if not the title; and an article by Theodosius Dobzhansky[4] provided the linchpin for the whole structure of bioethics in my mind. It was only after reading these three authors that I belatedly discovered Aldo Leopold, who had said so much so simply. I dedicated my book to him, although it contained no text-references to his work, hence my present emphasis on his views. I decided that biological wisdom (indeed, all wisdom) is a form of knowledge—"the knowledge of how to use knowledge for the social good"—and that "the search for wisdom should be organized and promoted in terms of the survival and improvement of the human species."[5] This, then, was the supra-ethical criterion called for by Waddington and it became the original bioethic, based on the idea that the imperative, Search for Wisdom! is an ethic in itself.

Theodosius Dobzhansky was a professor of zoology at Columbia University and had served as president of the American Society of Naturalists in 1951.[6] His 1956 book on *The Biological Basis of Human Freedom*[7] was listed by Waddington, but his 1958 article ("Evolution at Work") and its conclusions were not utilized. In 1958 Dobzhansky made three important points that influenced all of my subsequent thinking: (1) no biological law can be relied on to insure that our species will continue to prosper, or indeed that it will continue to exist; (2) the human species is the sole product of evolution that knows it has evolved and will continue to evolve; and (3) it is up to our collective wisdom to supply the program for "evolutionary developments that nature has failed to provide." The final proposal fits Waddington's supra-ethical criterion but it might well have been more modest. My own bioethic calls merely for an acceptable survival that would permit further evolution and development in view of Dobzhansky's claim that natural selection does not even guarantee that the species will endure; most biological species of the past have become extinct, without issue, and yet their evolution was controlled by natural selection. Their extinction occurred because "selection promotes what is immediately useful, even if the change may be fatal in the long run" (Dobzhansky 1958). If Dobzhansky's first two points are accepted as "what is," then "what ought to be" is a bioethic that permits the survival of generation after generation. The idea of *acceptable* survival (see chapter 2) is merely a refinement.

KNOWLEDGE OF ADAPTATION
IS NEEDED FOR WISDOM

The idea of survival is not a philosophic concept invented by modern ethicists. The bridge between knowledge of the "is" and the wisdom of the "ought" is the built-in program in every biological entity that makes it strive for survival beyond the existing generation. The mechanism for survival is based on the ability of a species to adapt to its environment. This is true even where humans modify the environment to their short-range needs. Adaptation is of three kinds. Individual members of a species, including humans, possess the property of *physiological adaptation.* Although bacteria and plants possess the property, it has not been documented for every species, and it may be that specialization to the exclusion of an adequate physiological adaptation is the first step on the road to extinction. Physiological adaptation occurs continually over minutes, hours, days or months in the lifetime of individual members of a species, without change in their genetic makeup. For example, adaptation to high altitude, which I have experienced and studied in the High Andes of Peru, occurs in several physiological systems with different time scales. Best known is the increase in hemoglobin and red cells in the blood. In all examples, built-in biocybernetic systems programmed by the DNA in the genetic apparatus constantly read the molecular and physical environments (for example, the percent of oxygen in the air) and feed back information to the machinery for genetic expression, changing the physiology of the individual in a seemingly purposeful (i.e., teleonomic) way to become as successful as possible in reproducing its genes into the next generation.[8]

Evolutionary adaptation is a property of a population. It occurs over a succession of generations by a gradual or sometimes rapid change in the genetic information stored in DNA as one generation succeeds another. The changes can be looked upon as copy-errors that are either spontaneous and infrequent or brought about more frequently by chemical or physical agents in the environment. Agents that cause copy-errors are usually damaging to individuals, causing cancer and other abnormalities at low concentrations and death at higher concentrations. Evolutionary adaptation may be seen as a mechanism for changing the capacity of a species to achieve descendents with improved physiological adaptation to a new environment or to the existing environment. It succeeds when changes in the environment are not too rapid.

If we attempt to define the "ought" from all this we find that every organism "knows" what is bad and what is good *for the present.* Anything that causes death without adequate species reproduction is bad. Anything that changes the genome in a way that diminishes the capacity for physiological adaptation to the range of environmental variations extant is bad. Anything that increases the capacity for physiological adaptation to the existing environment is good. But no organism is equipped to prepare in advance for a future altered environment (Dobzhansky 1958). Nevertheless, the human species may come closest to that possibility on the basis of its superior capacity for physiological and cultural adaptation. With cultural adaptation the possibility to escape extinction exists but cannot be guaranteed, even if an adequate overall bioethic could be adopted.

Cultural adaptation in humans and in a few species occurs both in individuals and in populations. It is limited by the two biological processes of adaptation, but it is speeded up tremendously by all the recent developments that can be lumped under the headings of *communication* and *information storage and retrieval*. It is possible that there are disadvantages to cultural adaptation that may be comparable to those in biological adaptation. That is, there is a fatal flaw in the combined biological mechanism such that, when a species becomes better and better adapted to a given steady-state environment, it may become totally incapable of surviving in an environment that has been drastically changed over a relatively short time period. So it may have been with the dinosaurs, as many believe. As noted earlier, most species that have ever existed have become extinct because of this fatal flaw in their genetic makeup. Until recently, the human species was no different from other species in the failure to see the fatal flaw. However, the human species now contains a few individuals who are aware of the significance of the fatal flaw. The propositions stated by Dobzhansky are less than thirty years old and to my knowledge have not been challenged. In fact, they would be regarded as truisms by most scientists who are knowledgeable in the field of evolution, even though they take no action in the matter. Of course, the creationists and any others who doubt that evolution is a fact of life are oblivious to the implications of the "fatal flaw."

Any ethic for the human species has to be based on the "is" of possible extinction and the fact that each of us has a built-in species-memory that tells us how we "ought" to live. We ought to live in such a way as to avoid the fate of most other species. We ought to listen to those few who have the knowledge that can contribute to the prevention or delay of extinction. We ought to develop interdisciplinary groups that can question those components of our present culture that are hastening the destruction of the natural environment. We ought to read Aldo Leopold and C. H. Waddington and consider whether our special knowledge can contribute to survival and amelioration of the human condition.

In this book I describe some of the urgent ethical problems that face society today. Dilemmas arise when decisions are demanded in the area covered by medical bioethics "when life takes precedence over health." The issue is basically one of deciding whether to adhere to the "sanctity of life" concept at all costs, or whether to raise the question of "quality of life" or "meaningful life." Medical technology has achieved miracles, yet in many cases the victory has been the thwarting of death but not the restoration of health. In other words, the new technologies frequently lead to decisions in which life maintenance has taken precedence over the restoration of a meaningful existence.

In the field of ecological bioethics there are also dilemmas that in some respects parallel the medical problems. The ambivalence of medical bioethics is mirrored in the powerlessness of ecological bioethics. For example, depletion and degradation of our water resources is the ecological equivalent of the neglect of the bioethical problem of teenage pregnancy by the medical profession. In both cases ethical theories abound but society has been unable to reach a consensus on what is to be done. Just as there are some medical bioethicists who argue for the maintenance of life no matter how miserable it may be, there are ecological bioethicists who argue that economic growth and full employment should have top priority, even at the cost of air and water pollution and accelerated depletion of nonrenewable resources. There is also a parallel between those who are arguing for meaningful life and those who are arguing for the preservation of the natural environment. Ecological bioethics must support the prevention of air and water pollution as well as the conservation of both renewable and nonrenewable resources. In essence, the issue is whether the quality of life concept is ethically similar to quality of the environment and whether the sanctity of life position has its counterpart in the sanctity of the dollar. Aldo Leopold recognized the latter position when he said,

> It of course goes without saying that economic feasibility limits the tether of what can or cannot be done for land. It always has and it always will. The fallacy the economic determinists have tied around our collective neck, and which we now need to cast off, is the belief that economics determines *all* land use. This is simply not true.[9]

Kenneth Boulding put it neatly when he said,

> Ecology's uneconomic,
> But with another kind of logic
> Economy's unecologic.[10]

Obviously we must seek a balance between ecological bioethics and economic domination just as we need to find a balance between sanctity of life and meaningful life.

Today it is apparent that many features of society, seen on a worldwide basis, are incompatible with acceptable survival or, to use Lester Brown's term, a "sustainable society" (see chap. 2). For many parts of the world, quality of life is a meaningless term; mere survival has become unpleasant and difficult. It is recognized that the goal of worldwide controlled human fertility on an equitable basis and within a healthy ecosystem may be impossible to achieve in a world with multiple ethnic and religious groups who oppose artificial means of birth control. However, without progress toward the achievement of the twin goals of birth control and environmental protection, the future could be bleak indeed.

We must therefore extend the present efforts in bioethics, particularly as they relate to medicine, to a recognition that the ethical behavior of humankind must be coherent with ecological realities. This exploration is an extension of ideas first formulated by Aldo Leopold. Only through the evolution of a third—and completely interdisciplinary and global—bioethics,[11] combining a reexamined medical bioethics with a responsibility-oriented ecological bioethics, can the future of humankind be seen as anything other than that foreseen by Robert Heilbroner in his introduction to *An Inquiry into the Human Prospect:* "The answer to whether we can conceive of the future other than as a continuation of the darkness, cruelty, and disorder of the past seems to be no; and to the question of whether worse impends, yes."[12]

---

1. Van Rensselaer Potter, *Bioethics, Bridge to the Future* (Englewood Cliffs, N.J.: Prentice-Hall, 1971). Chapter 1 was entitled "Bioethics, The Science of Survival," chapter 13 "Survival as a Goal for Wisdom," and chapter 12 "Biocybernetics—The Key to Environmental Science." Medical dilemmas were discussed in chapter 5, "Dangerous Knowledge: The Dilemma of Modern Science," and it was concluded that it is not dangerous knowledge but dangerous ignorance that we have to fear.
2. C. H. Waddington, *The Ethical Animal,* Phoenix Science Series (Chicago: University of Chicago Press, 1967), 19.
3. Margaret Mead. "Toward More Vivid Utopias," *Science* 126 (1957): 957–61.
4. Theodosius Dobzhansky, "Evolution at Work," *Science* 127 (1958): 1091–98.

5. Potter, "Survival as a Goal for Wisdom," chapter 13 in *Bioethics, Bridge to the Future*.

6. Theodosius Dobzhansky, in *Genetics in the 20th Century,* ed. L. C. Dunn (New York: Macmillan, 1951).

7. Theodosius Dobzhansky, *The Biological Basis of Human Freedom* (New York: Columbia University Press, 1956).

8. Van Rensselaer Potter, "Physiological Adaptation at the Molecular Level: The Frontier Where Research on Differentiation and Malignancy Meet," *Perspectives in Biology and Medicine* (Summer 1981): 525–42. I proposed that "the most significant aspect of the genetic program for differentiation is the development of a whole organism capable of 'physiological adaptation'. . . . I believe that research on physiological adaptation that combines the holistic and the reductionist approaches is the key to understanding differentiation and malignancy, and to my knowledge this point has not been previously made, although it is implicit in much current research which describes *what* happens without commenting on *why* it happens."

9. Aldo Leopold, *A Sand County Almanac* (New York: Oxford University Press, 1949, 1966; reprint ed., New York: Sierra Club/Ballantine Books, 1970), 262.

10. Kenneth Boulding, in *Future Environments in North America,* ed. F. Fraser Darling and John P. Milton (Garden City, N.Y.: The Natural History Press, 1966), 717. An important symposium.

11. A global bioethic is not unique to the writer. There are over 100 U.S. citizens' organizations whose efforts are primarily directed toward the twin issues of population and environment in varying proportions. Nearly all are members of the Global Tomorrow Coalition at 1325 G Street, N.W., Suite 1003, Washington, D.C. 20005. Most of the organizations have primarily a national operation although they have a global outlook. A major group, formerly The Environmental Fund has changed its name to Population-Environment Balance, and is at the same address. Zero Population Growth (ZPG) is at 1601 Connecticut Ave., N.W., Washington, D.C. 20009, and Negative Population Growth (NPG) is at 16 East 42nd St., Suite 1042, New York, N.Y. 10017.

12. Robert L. Heilbroner, *An Inquiry into the Human Prospect* (New York: W. W. Norton, 1974). The author examined "the ecological aspect" and the problem of "population overload" within a broad framework. Perhaps the single most important, concise, recent book.

1

THE LEOPOLD LEGACY

WHEN ALDO LEOPOLD WROTE "The Land Ethic," published in 1948 but developed over a number of years, he expressed a concern which is still applicable today: "Perhaps the most serious obstacle impeding the evolution of a land ethic is the fact that our educational and economic system is headed away from, rather than toward, an intense consciousness of land."[1] By land, he meant "not merely soil; it is a fountain of energy flowing through a circuit of soils, plants, and animals" (216). This book is, in part, an attempt to reaffirm and promote precepts and values such as these which were the sum and substance of Leopold's land ethic.

Aldo Leopold began his highly motivated and creative career as a professional forester. His interests continually widened as he became a conservationist, ecologist, administrator, lecturer, writer, philosopher, and poetic spirit. In her work on the life and accomplishments of Leopold "and the evolution of an ecological attitude toward deer, wolves and forests," Susan Flader traces the evolution and adaptation of Leopold from his early experiences as a forester to his final position at the University of Wisconsin in Madison.[2]

No sooner had Leopold received his first job as a forester in the Southwest (Arizona and New Mexico, in 1909) than he began to break out of the forestry specialty and to propose a new discipline combining forestry with what he called "game management." He felt impelled, somewhat as Martin Luther did, to announce his convictions by nailing them to the cathedral door, in this case the *Journal of Forestry*. In 1918 he wrote an article entitled "Forestry and Game Conservation" in which he made his position clear: "In conclusion, the writer is sensible of the fact that in *arraigning* the profession of forestry for a *passive attitude* toward the game problem, he speaks from the standpoint of a game conservation enthusiast" (italics added).[3] While he spoke of the "game problem" and of game conservation, he immediately followed by asking, "But why, indeed, should not more foresters likewise be enthusiasts on this question? They should—in fact, they must be, if they are to act as leaders in launching *the new science of game management*" (italics added). In 1933 Leopold published his epic textbook *Game Management,*[4] which "is still regarded as a basic statement of the science, art, and profession of wildlife management" and which "has been continuously in print since 1933" (Flader, 23). While this authoritative textbook, which created the new science of game management, integrated the details from 427 sources by my count, only seven were from the *Journal of Forestry* and three of those were by Leopold himself. Interestingly enough, he did not refer to his 1918 proposal that foresters must act as leaders in the new science.

With the publication in 1933 of *Game Management,* Leopold might have become trapped in a process of revision that never ends for most authors as long as the later editions find readers. Not so with Leopold. His book was reprinted but not revised, because he turned his creative writing talents to the wider meaning of conservation. As in the case of his criticism of specialized forestry, he now criticized academic specialization, even though he himself had created a new specialty. Leopold called the reductionist approach used by specialists in the university system "dismemberment," criticizing professors for "examining the construction of the plants, animals, and soils which are the instruments of the great orchestra" without ever looking for the "harmony" (*Almanac,* 153). Leopold's expanding vision called for an understanding of the whole field of ecology, a specialty combining all biological specialties; but he wanted to go even further. He concluded with the somewhat bitter remark that the scientist, like the otter playing tag in the pools and riffles of the Gavilan, "has no doubts about his own design for living. He assumes that for him the Gavilan will sing forever" (154).

NEW PERSPECTIVES ON THE LEOPOLD LEGACY

The most illuminating picture of Aldo Leopold and a magnificent monument to him is the thoroughly researched and authoritative biography *Aldo Leopold. His Life and Work,* published by Curt Meine in 1988.[5] Meine spent over three years working with hundreds of letters, as well as the original notes and journals of Leopold preserved in the Leopold archives at the University of Wisconsin, along with personal interviews, published and unpublished manuscripts, and other historical sources to give us the first comprehensive biography of Aldo Leopold. Not the least useful portion of the coverage is the complete list of the "Published Writings of Aldo Leopold" (603–20) covering the years 1911 to 1948, for which Meine gives Susan Flader "principal credit for its compilation." From this list we learn that during the years 1933 to 1948, when Leopold was compiling the essays which eventually gave birth to "The Land Ethic," he was issuing a barrage of short papers on a bewildering variety of subjects in a plethora of communication channels, each message articulating a particular aspect of his many-faceted world views. For example, in 1940, when he first published "Song of the Gavilan" (later included in the *Almanac*), he published twenty-three other items on various topics in sixteen different media channels, of which *Wisconsin Agriculturist and Farmer* contained six and *Journal of Wildlife Management* contained five, while the others contained one or two by my count. A similar tally for the entire period of 1911–1948, with an attempt to categorize the topics covered, would only begin to plumb the dimensions of the Leopold legacy. The many citations from his early letters to his mother and father also reveal a new insight into Leopold's lifelong love of nature. In short, the Meine book contains encyclopedic coverage of the Leopold legacy, including reference to earlier books on Leopold.

On a much smaller scale than Meine's work is another book from the University of Wisconsin Press entitled *Companion to A Sand County Almanac*.[6] Edited by J. Baird Callicott, it contains thirteen essays by ten authors to provide well-organized coverage. The 1986–88 harvest included additional insights by Wisconsin professors Jon N. Moline[7] and Robert A. McCabe, [8] a student of Aldo Leopold.

From such a wealth of material it is my impression that Leopold contributed so much to so many aspects of conservation that his underlying concern for the future of the human species was overlooked. His views on the overconsumption of renewable and nonrenewable resources by an exponentially increasing human population were neglected, while his love of nature was a comfortable aspect of his life for others to assimilate.

Yet Leopold did worry about consumption of material goods and, indeed, was the first to enunciate the concept of zero population growth (ZPG). In a minor publication (*Condor*) in 1932, he responded to some criticism in a two-page commentary on all of his admitted personal depletions of the natural environment:

> "Nay more, *when I father more than two children* I am creating an insatiable need for more printing presses, more cows, more coffee, more oil, and more rubber, to supply which more birds, more trees, and more flowers will either be killed, or what is just as destructive, evicted from their environments." (Meine, 290, italics added)

ALDO LEOPOLD'S NEGLECTED LEGACY

Aldo Leopold saw that human survival depended on the maintenance of a healthy ecosystem and the control of human fertility—at a time when neither of these ideas was widely understood. I believe he was able to define right and wrong ultimately in terms of human survival and the preservation of the biosphere. "A thing is right when it tends to preserve the integrity, stability, and beauty of the biotic community. It is wrong when it tends otherwise" (*Almanac,* 224).

Leopold laid out a coherent and logical sequence of propositions that contains much more than that simple statement, which has been taken by many to encompass the Leopold philosophy. It seems justifiable to conclude that he was indeed concerned with the relation between increases in the human population and the "permanence" or survival of society. He felt that the human species can survive only if (1) the ecosystem as a whole is capable of recovering and surviving the "violence" exercised by the human species in the course of economic exploitation; and (2) the number of human beings is held within the boundaries set by the limitations of the ecosystem. If these conclusions were apparent to an ecologist in 1933, what should ecologists of the 1980s conclude? Perhaps a review of Leopold's views could open the discussion.

From Leopold's "Land Ethic" (*Almanac,* 201–26), we can distill a series of statements that could be regarded as axiomatic and self-evident by anyone who has had sufficient experience in the field of ecology and who is concerned with the survival of humankind in a healthy ecosystem. I will refer to these statements collectively as "A Leopold Primer." I do not believe that a comparable synoptic view of "The Land Ethic" is available. I have quoted directly or paraphrased twenty-four Leopold statements under three headings: Land, Ethics, and Survival. Each statement in the first two instances is based on a sentence in which Leopold used the word *land* or the word *ethic.* In the third instance I have inferred that *survival* was in Leopold's mind. It is not implied that the statements, either in the original form or as paraphrased, are statements of fact; they are value judgments from Leopold, a man with a deep and profound ecological conscience. It is recommended that readers examine the original context.

A LEOPOLD PRIMER

I. Land

    1. The basic concept of ecology is that land is a community. (Paraphrased from 204)

    2. "Land then, is not merely soil; it is a fountain of energy flowing through a circuit of soils, water, plants, and animals [and back] to the soil." (216)

    3. Land, collectively, is a biotic mechanism. (Paraphrased from 214)

    4. "Many historical events, hitherto explained solely in terms of human enterprise, were actually biotic interactions between people and land." (205)

II. Ethics

    5. "An ethic, ecologically, is a limitation on freedom of action in the struggle for existence." (202)

    6. "An ethic, philosophically, is a differentiation of social from anti-social conduct." (202)

    7. "There is as yet no ethic dealing with man's relation to land and to the animals and plants which grow upon it." (203)

    8. "The extension of ethics to [land] is an evolutionary possibility and an ecological necessity [for human survival]." (203)

    9. "All ethics so far evolved rest upon a single premise: that the individual is a member of a community of interdependent parts." (203)

    10. "A land ethic changes the role of *Homo sapiens* from conqueror of the land-community to plain member and citizen of it." (204)

    11. "[A land ethic] implies respect [by human individuals for their fellow humans] and also respect for the [biotic] community as such." (204)

    12. "A land ethic . . . reflects the existence of an ecological conscience." (221)

    13. "An ethic to supplement and guide the economic relationship to land presupposes the existence of some mental image of land as a biotic mechanism." (214)

14. "We can be ethical only in relation to something we can see, feel, understand, love, or otherwise have faith in." (214)

15. "Individual thinkers, since the days of Ezekiel and Isaiah, have asserted that the despoliation of land is not only inexpedient but wrong." (203)

III. Survival

16. "Man-made changes [in the land-community] are of a different order than evolutionary changes, and have effects more comprehensive than is intended or foreseen." (218)

17. "The less violent the man-made changes, the greater the probability of successful readjustment" [in the biotic community]. (220)

18. "Violence [to the biotic community] varies with human population density; a dense population requires a more violent conversion." (220)

19. "North America has a better chance for permanence [survival] than Europe if she can contrive to limit her population density." (220)

20. "Ecology knows of no population density relationship that holds for indefinitely wide limits. All gains from density are subject to a law of diminishing returns." (220)

21. "Many biotas ... have already exceeded their sustained carrying capacity. Most of South America is overpopulated in this sense." (219)

22. Decent land use requires decisions based on what is ethically and esthetically right, as well as what is economically expedient. (Paraphrased from 224)

23. "An ethic may be regarded as a mode of guidance for meeting ecological situations so new or intricate, or involving such deferred reactions, that the path of social expediency is not discernible to the average individual." (203)

24. "A thing is right when it tends to preserve the integrity, stability, and beauty of the biotic community. It is wrong when it tends otherwise." (224–25)

The final statement (No. 24) may well be the most famous and most discussed quotation from Leopold. One of his daughters, Nina Leopold Bradley, has commented on how this ethic affected Leopold's whole family.[9] The statement has been called "the categorical imperative or principal precept of the land ethic" by Callicott[10] I have referred to it as "the Leopold Imperative.[11] Callicott has also remarked that Leopold's land ethic "has become a modern classic and may be treated as the standard example—the paradigm case, as it were—of what an environmental ethic is" (54). Callicott then extrapolates from Leopold's statement into a discussion of animal liberation, animal rights, plant rights, landscape rights, and all of the literature of that genre, without considering the issue of the survival of the human species in acceptable form, which I have taken to be the thrust of Leopold's entire message if we consider all of the statements presented above. Callicott concludes, "In every case the effect upon ecological systems is the decisive factor in the determination of the ethical quality actions" (61). He seems to assume that Leopold was more concerned with plant and animal rights than with human interests, citing many of the romantic passages from Leopold's writings.

These passages help us to understand Leopold the naturalist, but in my opinion the land ethic was not an either/or choice of human rights versus plant and animal rights. Rather, it expressed the belief that the human species cannot survive without "a capacity to see, feel, understand, love, or otherwise have faith" in the land community (No. 14).

Like Carol Gilligan (see chapter 4), Leopold was concerned more with responsibilities than with rights. When Leopold referred to carrying capacity (No. 21), surely he had in mind carrying capacity for people, plants, and animals. Leopold was concerned about the violence to the biotic community and the disastrous effects of increased population density (No. 18). It seems inappropriate to equate Leopold's land ethic with romantic passages outside the section bearing that name. In the *Almanac* and in *The Quality of Landscape* we see how much Leopold loved Nature, while in "The Land Ethic" we see how Leopold came at last to see that unless what he loved could be protected, the fate of humankind would be in doubt. Twenty-nine years before *Silent Spring,* he wisely noted that "man-made changes . . . have effects more comprehensive than is intended or foreseen" (No. 16). Hence, "an ethic may be regarded as a mode of guidance for meeting ecological situations so new or intricate, or involving such deferred reactions, that the path of social expediency for humankind's survival is not discernible to the average individual" (No. 23).

There is nothing illogical about placing value on a healthy ecosystem for *two* reasons: for its intrinsic value, if we have sufficient experience and insight or if we can be taught to see it; and for its instrumental value, as the home in which humankind has evolved and in which the species must continue to live. I insist that when Leopold speaks of obligations over and above self-interest he refers to the self-interest of individuals, corporations, and governments here and now, while obligations to the "land" are obligations and responsibilities to future generations of the human species, obligations that can be fulfilled only when sufficient numbers of humans here and now can learn to "see, feel, understand, love, or otherwise have faith in" the land, whether they love it for instrumental or noninstrumental reasons. "A land ethic implies respect by human individuals for their fellow humans and also respect for the biotic community as such" (No. 11).

Aldo Leopold believed that the human species is and always will be dependent on the plants and animals that in turn depend on the soil, water and air in the natural environment. He also believed that the natural environment could not be maintained in a condition compatible with the health and survival of the human species if the human population increased its numbers indefinitely. Leopold had observed the effect of overpopulation of deer in the Southwest, which led to his essay "Thinking Like a Mountain" (*Almanac,* 129–33). Leopold used the actual term "overpopulation" in an article published in 1947 in the *Journal of Wildlife Management:* "A Survey of Overpopulated Deer Ranges in the United States." He foresaw the time when overgrazing and deforestation would lead to "the flood that one day will scour the bank into the Pacific" (*Almanac,* 154). It is this side of Leopold which I believe has been neglected.

In early 1987 my wife and I happened to see a copy of William Vogt's *Road to Survival*[12] at a used book sale and bought it for 50 cents. It was still in its original dust jacket, and what should I see on the back cover, listed among "What advance readers have said," but a testimonial from Aldo Leopold:

ALDO LEOPOLD—

> *"This book is the most lucid analysis of human ecology and land use that I have yet encountered. It is as dramatic and as absorbing as any piece of fiction and what is more it is written by a keen-minded scientist who knows his facts thoroughly. I hope every thoughtful man and woman in this atomic age will read it."*

I thought, how poignant: Leopold praised the book but lost his life in a tragic fire just as Vogt's book was released in 1948 and before his own book was off the press.

I wondered if Vogt and Leopold had been acquainted. Where to look? I thought of Curt Meine, whose biography of Aldo Leopold was then in press. I called him and he obligingly sent me xerox copies of relevant pages from his manuscript, here cited from the book.

Reading from his epic work, I found the "Vogt-Leopold Connection." Meine noted that following the end of the war, people began to consider the path ahead. He wrote:

> Leopold participated in a number of these discussions. Among his many constant correspondents at this time, the most significant was Bill Vogt. Vogt had spent the war years in Latin America as Chief of the Conservation Section of the twenty-one-nation Pan American Union. In that capacity he surveyed the natural resources and wartime social conditions across Latin America. What he saw—the cluster of unconscionable poverty, resource exploitation, burgeoning populations, unresponsive oligarchies, and an unyielding Roman Catholic stance on birth control—transformed him from an already brilliant ornithologist and writer to a conservationist with a mission. By early 1946, he was laying the groundwork for an "Inter-American Conservation Congress."
>
> Vogt and Leopold had known one another for a decade, and for a time Vogt planned to study under Leopold at Wisconsin [he was about twelve years younger] but the plan fell through. At another point, Vogt tried to bring Leopold south on a lecture tour. "The importance of introducing ecology into the South American picture is so obvious that it needs no comment," Vogt wrote to him in 1942. "From what I know of Latin America, their problems [and] you and your approach to such problems, I cannot help feeling that such a journey would result in extremely important accomplishments, both in the field of hemisphere science and its relations to strategic problems." Aldo was never able to make such a trip. . . .

After the war, Vogt was determined to bring his dire message to the public. As envisioned, the Inter-American Conservation Congress was to be the first large-scale forum on Latin American environmental conditions and would require several years to organize. In January 1946, Vogt sent to Leopold an early outline of the proposed conference. Leopold's response was gloomy:

"The only thing you have left out is whether the philosophy of industrial cultures is not, in its ultimate development, irreconcilable with ecological conservation. I think it is.

"I hasten to add, however, that the term industrialism cannot be used as an absolute. Like 'temperature' and 'velocity' it is a question of degree. Throughout ecology, all truth is relative: a thing becomes good at one degree and ceases to be so at another.

"Industrialism might theoretically be conservative if there were an ethic limiting its application to what does not impair (a) permanence and stability of the land, (b) beauty of the land. But there is no such ethic, nor likely to be. . . .

"Bill, your outline is excellent. That the situation is hopeless should not prevent us from doing our best."

Even Vogt, who could hardly be called an optimist, found Leopold's forecast "somewhat dismal but much appreciated." Vogt could not deny Leopold's main point. "You are, of course, correct in what you say about industrialism. I don't know how you would define ethic, but I am hopeful that horse sense may someday replace it as a limiting factor to preserve the permanence and stability of the land, even though there seems to be little hope for saving its beauty." Leopold was no doubt depressed by the trend of world events, but, as in the past, he always surfaced with his thoughts pointed toward the future. He wrote to Vogt a week later: "It is so impossible to write a letter about such a big question that I am afraid this alone depresses anyone trying to make an answer." . . .

There were other reflections of the broadening conservation movement in Leopold's life throughout 1946. He served that year as chairman of a new

Committee on Foreign Relations within the Wildlife Society. In his first draft resolution to the Committee members, Leopold stated that "this Committee wishes to assert flatly its belief that provincialism is as dangerous in the wildlife field as in any other." (477–80)

Turning now to Bill Vogt's book we read his reference to Leopold's study of overpopulation among deer:

In the Kaibab forest on the north rim of the Grand Canyon, thoroughgoing government predator control was followed by an increase in the mule deer population from four thousand to one hundred thousand in *fourteen years.* Consumption of all browse within reach was followed, in two years, by a 60 percent reduction in the herd through starvation [Reference to Leopold, *Journal of Wildlife Management,* 1947]. (Vogt, 90)

Under "The Rewards of Understanding" we read:

The sheer intellectual and emotional satisfaction to be had from understanding—really seeing—the countryside is a privilege within reach of anyone. By failing to show us the way to it, our schools deprive us not only of a great and lifelong gratification but of the comprehension that should guide all our relations to our environment. The fortunate people who have been afield with such a teacher as Homer L. Shantz, Aldo Leopold, or Isaiah Bowman not only are going to find excitement and satisfaction in living; they are going to be much more useful citizens in a world that desperately needs them. Unless we rapidly adjust our demands and uses to the complex of land limitations and potentialities, the human race is going to suffer such travail as it has never known. (Vogt, 95)

Finally, opening chapter 7 "The Land on Edge" we read:

> All Latin American countries except three or four
> are overpopulated. They are able to feed and shelter
> their citizens, and supply water for their many
> needs, only by a progressive and accelerating
> destruction of natural resources; biological bank-
> ruptcy hangs over their heads like a shaking ava-
> lanche. . . . Unless there is a profound modification
> in its treatment of the land, the greater part of
> Mexico will be a desert within one hundred years.
> (Vogt, 152)

Now we know how it was that Leopold came to his
conclusion on the overpopulation of South America
(No. 21).

I hope it will become apparent that a common
thread exists among Vogt, Leopold, and others like
Gregg and Berrill whom I will mention later. This
common thread is a concern about human survival,
and it is what constitutes the Leopold connection to
the twenty-first century. Although Leopold's concern with human survival seems clear enough from
his writing, it is not this aspect of his land ethic that
is emphasized. Even in the most recent publications
the emphasis is on his personhood and his love of
nature. Only Wallace Stegner mentions the population problem in terms of the consequences: "Less
green, less space, less freedom, less health; a longer
and longer stretching of a rubberband not indefinitely stretchable."[13] Yet even he does not reach the
conclusion that the end result of overpopulation is
miserable survival and death, as Leopold witnessed
for the deer in New Mexico.

This book, rooted in the philosophy of Aldo
Leopold, will explore the urgency of its relevance to
the dilemmas of our time.

1. Aldo Leopold, "The Land Ethic," *A Sand County Almanac* (New York: Oxford University Press, Inc., 1949, 1966; reprint., New York: Sierra Club/Ballantine Books, 1970, with eight essays from *Round River*; reissued in a special Commemorative Edition by Oxford, 1987), 223. The page references herein are from the 1987 edition.

2. Susan Flader, *Thinking Like a Mountain. Aldo Leopold and the Evolution of an Ecological Attitude Toward Deer, Wolves, and Forests* (Lincoln: University of Nebraska Press, 1978).

3. Aldo Leopold, "Forestry and Game Management," *Journal of Forestry* 16: (1918): 404–11.

4. Aldo Leopold, *Game Management* (New York: Scribners, 1933).

5. Curt Meine, *Aldo Leopold. His Life and Work* (Madison: University of Wisconsin Press, 1988), 529 pages of text and photographs plus 105 pages of bibliographies, notes, and index.

6. J. Baird Callicott, ed., *Companion to A Sand County Almanac* (Madison: University of Wisconsin Press, 1987).

7. Jon N. Moline, "Aldo Leopold and the Moral Community," *Environmental Ethics* 8 (Summer 1986): 99–120.

8. Robert A. McCabe, *Aldo Leopold, The Professor* (Madison: Rusty Rock Press, 1987).

9. Nina Leopold Bradley, letter to the author 3 March 1988. "An action policy to help guide his own children was Leopold's restoration of his worn out sand county farm. With enthusiasm from his wife and five children (later in his life he spoke of the impropriety of siring more than two children) the family learned a good deal about the land organism as they tried to rebuild 'integrity, stability and beauty' into it. The simplicity of the 'Shack,' the hard work with shovel and axe, the camaraderie, the love of land, brought us to a wider understanding of each other, of the natural system, and our place in it."

10. J. Baird Callicott, "Animal Liberation: A Triangular Affair," in *Ethics and the Environment,* ed. D. Scherer and T. Attig (Englewood Cliffs, N.J.: Prentice-Hall, 1983).

11. V. R. Potter, "Bioethics and the Human Prospect," in *Studies in Science and Culture,* vol. 1, *The Culture of Biomedicine,* ed. D. H. Brook (Cranbury, N.J.: Asso-ciaiton of University Presses, Inc., 1984), 124-37.
12. William Vogt, *Road to Survival* (New York: William Sloane Associates, Inc., 1948).
13. Wallace Stegner, "The Legacy of Aldo Leopold," in Callicott, *Companion,* 239.

2

HUMAN SURVIVAL

THE CANCER ANALOGY

ON DECEMBER 28, 1954, the American Association for the Advancement of Science held a symposium on "Population Problems," at which Dr. Alan Gregg, vice-president of the Rockefeller Foundation (1951–56), came up with a startling idea: the thought that the human species is to the planet Earth what a cancer is to an individual human being. As a cancer specialist I was aware of the many contributing lines of thought and so was not altogether surprised to note the same idea proposed by another eminent biologist, Professor Norman J. Berrill of McGill University, in his superb book *Man's Emerging Mind.*[1] It was published in 1955, the same year that Gregg's symposium paper appeared in *Science.*[2] The remarks by these two men of science suggest that the effect of an ever-expanding human population on the carrying-capacity of the planet Earth bears examination. We do would well to examine their words.

EARTH AS ORGANISM

Gregg espoused an idea that was clearly enunciated in 1949 by Aldo Leopold, who referred to
"land the collective organism" and stated, "Land,
then, is not merely soil; it is a fountain of energy
flowing through a circuit of soils, plants, and animals. Food chains are the living channels which
conduct energy upward; death and decay return it
to the soil."[3] Leopold also anticipated Gregg and
Berrill when he remarked, "This almost worldwide
display of disorganization in the land seems to be
similar to disease in an animal except that it never
culminates in complete disorganization or death.
The land recovers, but at some reduced level of
complexity, and with a reduced carrying capacity
for people, plants, and animals" (*Almanac,* 297).

Alan Gregg proposed similar ideas in his aforementioned symposium paper: "If we regard the different forms of plant and animal life in the world as
being so closely related to and dependent on one
another that they resemble different types of cells in
a total organism, then we may, for the sake of a
hypothesis, consider the living world as an organism." He went on to say,

> What would we think if it became evident that
> within a very brief period in the history of the
> world some one type of its forms of life had
> increased greatly at the expense of other types of
> life? In short, I suggest, as a way of looking at the
> population problem, that there are some interesting
> analogies between the growth of the human popu-
> lation of the world and the increase of cells observ-
> able in neoplasms. To say that the world has cancer,
> and that the cancer cell is man has neither experi-
> mental proof nor the validation of predictive accu-
> racy; but I see no reason that instantly forbids such
> a speculation. . . . Cancerous growths demand
> food; but, so far as I know, they have never been

cured by getting it. . . . How nearly the slums of our great cities resemble the necrosis of tumors raises the whimsical query: which is the more offensive to decency and beauty, slums or the fetid detritus of a growing tumor? . . . If Copernicus helped astronomy by challenging the geocentric interpretation of the universe, might it not help biology to challenge the anthropocentric interpretation of nature?

Norman Berrill was in complete agreement with Leopold and Gregg. In "The Human Crop," chapter 17 of *Man's Emerging Mind,* he discussed the issue at length:

Directly or indirectly there has been a monumental and increasingly extensive conversion of the planet's living potential from the diverse many to the all-consuming one. In terms of our comparison, the virgin prairie with its stable mixture of grasses and flowers has become almost entirely corn, with a few weeds and some blowing dust. All that can be transformed into human protoplasm is being transformed, and anything that stands in the way is pushed against the wall. . . . So far as the rest of nature is concerned we are like a cancer whose strange cells multiply without restraint, ruthlessly demanding the nourishment that all of the body has need of. The analogy is not far-fetched for cancer cells no more than whole organisms know when to stop multiplying, and sooner or later the body or the community is starved of support and dies. (209–10)

Berrill saw three possible responses to the problem of overpopulation.

One is that we can increase our resources indefinitely to keep pace with the increasing population, which I have tried to show is impossible. Another is that we employ our collective intelligence and keep our numbers within reasonable bounds, while the

third is the pessimistic one that human beings are
not intelligent enough as a whole to control their
own fertility and will always press hard against the
ragged fringe of sustenance . . . that always the
more fertile or the more prolific human strains or
races will outbreed the rest, that population control
by any group sooner or later seals its own doom,
with those who retain an uncontrollable breeding
instinct taking its place. (220–21)

The analogy that sees Earth as an organism with
all living species as cells in that organism is not complete in detail because the various species exist by
and large by consuming the bodies, living or dead,
of other species. In contrast, the cells that form an
organism in the human body do not live by consuming other cells in the community, although the
total human organism does depend on the intake of
plant and animal species as food. Nevertheless, the
proliferation of cell types within a human organism
is exquisitely regulated by feedback mechanisms of
great complexity, and the same can be said for the
proliferation of living species on the planet Earth. In
either case, when "some one type of its forms of life
had increased greatly at the expense of other types
of life," to use Gregg's words, we must conclude
that the natural feedback mechanisms, evolved over
millions of years, have broken down. It becomes
clear that in either case the result is brought about
by a great excess of births over the number of
deaths in a given time interval. If the human species
is to survive and prosper, it is essential that we must
control not only nuclear armaments but also human
fertility and the tendency to crowd out or destroy
other forms of life. This statement of "what we must
do" is merely an extension of the concluding
Leopold Paradigm: "A thing [referring to decent
land use] is right when it tends to preserve the

integrity, stability, and beauty of the biotic community. It is wrong when it tends to do otherwise" (see chapter 1).

THE ISSUE OF SURVIVAL

It was perhaps Garrett Hardin more than any other who independently developed the equivalent of the Leopold paradigms and realized that this led directly to the issue of fertility control for the human population. In 1968 he wrote "The Tragedy of the Commons" in which he concluded that "freedom to breed is intolerable."[4] In 1972 he went beyond Leopold when he wrote, "With the flowering of concern for environmental quality and the growth of theory in ecology the time is now ripe, I think, for a concerted attack on the population-environment-quality complex. I think it is almost time to grasp the nettle of population control, which we sometime must, if we are to survive with dignity."[5] With that statement he began what I propose to continue, that is, the adoption of the criterion of survival as a guide for action, and the discussion of what kind of survival we should advocate.

Like Garrett Hardin, Eugene P. Odum, co-author of *Fundamentals of Ecology,* was concerned with the relation between population and survival. Quoting extensively from Leopold's views on the need to extend ethics to the relation of man to the natural environment, Odum wrote: "We can also present strong scientific and technological reasons for the proposition that such a major extension of the general theory of ethics is now necessary for human survival."[6] Like Gregg and Berrill he noted the cancer analogy: "Growth beyond the optimum becomes cancer. Cancer is an ever-present threat to any mature system and must constantly be guarded against."[7] In proposing "The Emergence of Ecology as a New Integrative Discipline" in 1977,[8] he quoted Alex Novikoff on reductionism and holism: "Equally essential for the purposes of scientific analysis are both the isolation of parts of a whole and their integration into the structure of the whole. . . . The consideration of one to the exclusion of the other acts to retard the development of biological and sociological sciences."[9] Odum concluded: "To achieve a truly holistic or ecosystematic approach, not only ecology but other disciplines in the natural, social, and political sciences as well must emerge to new hitherto unrecognized and unresearched levels of thinking and action" ("Emergence of Ecology," 1291), echoing Hardin's plea for "a concerted attack on the population-environment-quality complex."

When Richard Falk of Princeton University wrote *This Endangered Planet: Prospects and Proposals for Human Survival* (1971), he discussed the four dimensions of planetary danger as: (1) the war system; (2) population pressure; (3) insufficiency of resources; and (4) environmental overload. Following Paul Shepard, who in turn had paid tribute to Rachel Carson and Aldo Leopold, Falk reflected Odum's views when he wrote:

> Such a posture of concern and position makes of human ecology a kind of ethics of survival. It is a science that relies on careful procedures of inquiry, data collection, and detailed observation as the basis of inference, explanation, and prediction. But it also involves a moral commitment to survival and to the enhancement of the natural habitat of man.[10]

All of the above authors have seen a link between ecology, population pressure, and human survival. They have in general not considered what survival. They have in general not considered what kind of survival, although Hardin spoke of surviving "with dignity" and Berrill visualized humankind always pressing hard against "the ragged fringe of sustenance." Unlike the vast majority of the human species, they are aware that humankind has no guarantee of survival, that survival cannot be assumed.

SURVIVAL CANNOT BE ASSUMED

In 1967–70, I was a member of a group of university professors in an Interdisciplinary Studies Committee on the Future of Man. We published a report on the "Purpose and Function of the University," subtitled "University scholars have a major responsibility for survival and quality of life in the future."[11] In this report we stated,

> We affirm the views that the survival of civilized man is not something to be taken for granted, that governments throughout the world are experiencing great difficulty in planning for the future while trying to cope with the present, and finally, that the university is one of the institutions that has a major responsibility for the survival and improvement of life for civilized man.

My book, *Bioethics, Bridge to the Future,*[12] commented on the need for a new synthesis:

> Mankind is urgently in need of new wisdom that will provide the "knowledge of how to use knowledge" for man's survival and for improvement in the quality of life. This concept of wisdom as a guide for action—the knowledge of how to use knowledge for the social good—might be called *Science of Survival,* surely the prerequisite to improvement in the quality of life. I take the position that the science of survival must be built on the

science of biology and enlarged beyond the traditional boundaries to include the most essential elements of the social sciences and the humanities with emphasis on philosophy in the strict sense, meaning "love of wisdom." A science of survival must be more than science alone, and I therefore propose the term *Bioethics* in order to emphasize the two most important ingredients in achieving the new wisdom that is so desperately needed: biological knowledge and human values.

In this age of specialization we seem to have lost contact with the daily reminders that must have driven home the truth to our ancestors: man cannot live without harvesting plants or killing animals. If plants wither and die and animals fail to reproduce, man will sicken and die and fail to maintain his kind. As individuals we cannot afford to leave our destiny in the hands of scientists, engineers, technologists, and politicians who have forgotten or who never knew these simple truths. In our modern world we have botanists who study plants and zoologists who study animals, but most of them are specialists who do not deal with the ramifications of their limited knowledge. Today we need biologists who respect the fragile web of life and who can broaden their knowledge to include the nature of man and his relation to the biological and physical worlds. We need biologists who can tell us what we can and must do to survive and what we cannot and must not do if we hope to maintain and improve the quality of life during the next three decades. *The fate of the world rests on the integration, preservation, and extension of the knowledge that is possessed by a relatively small number of people who are only just beginning to realize how inadequate their strength, how enormous the task* [italics added]. Every college student owes it to society to learn as much as possible of what these leaders have to offer, to challenge them, to meld biological knowledge with whatever additional ingredient they are able to master, and to become, if their talents are adequate, the new leaders of tomorrow. From such a pooling of knowledge and values may come a new kind of scholar or statesman who has mastered what I have referred to as Bioethics. No individual could possibly master all of the components of this branch of knowledge, just as no one today knows all of zoology or all of chemistry. What is needed is a new discipline to provide models of life styles for people who can communicate with each other and propose and explain the new public policies that could provide a "bridge to the future." The new disciplines will be forged in the heat of today's crisis problems, all of which require some kind of a mix between basic biology, social sciences, and the humanities.

Biology is more than botany and zoology. It is the foundation on which we build *ecology,* which is the relation among plants, animals, man, and the physical environment. Biology includes the science of genetics, which has to do with all aspects of heredity, and physiology, which deals with the function of individuals. For thousands of years men have lived on this earth with no generally disseminated knowledge of their chemical nature. Man's dependence upon his natural environment was widely understood, but Nature's bounty was considered to be limitless and Nature's capacity to recover from exploitation was considered to be ample. Eventually it was realized that man was exploiting the earth to an extent that required the use of more and more science and technology as the richest sources of iron and copper, for example, were used up. From the biological standpoint man has progressively taken over the planet's resources by decreasing the numbers and kinds of other species of life and by increasing only those species that were useful to man, such as wheat, beef cattle, and other consumables. . . .

From many uninformed quarters we now hear demands for a moratorium on science, when what we need is more and better science. We need to combine biology with humanistic knowledge from diverse sources and forge a science of survival that will be able to set a system of priorities. We need to start action in the areas where knowledge is already available, and we need to reorient our research effort to get the necessary knowledge if it is not available.

The age-old questions about the nature of man[cf. Trosko][13] and his relation to the world become increasingly important as we approach the remaining three decades in this century, when political decisions made in ignorance of biological knowledge, or in defiance of it, may jeopardize man's future and indeed the future of earth's biological resources for human needs. As individuals we speak of the "instinct for survival," but the sum total of all our individual instincts for survival is not enough to guarantee the survival of the human race in a form that any of us would willingly accept. An *instinct* for survival is not enough. We must develop the *science* of survival, and it must start with a new kind of ethics—bioethics. (1–3)

Having agreed with all those who expressed concern for human survival, and having concluded that ecological bioethics is a key ingredient in attempts to ensure survival, we must now consider what we mean by survival.

THE MEANING OF SURVIVAL

Until recently it has always been assumed that survival of the human species could be taken for granted; the question of whether survival is something to be desired was accordingly not an issue. When Charles Darwin wrote *The Origin of Species* in 1859, he was optimistic about the future of humankind. He wrote in his penultimate paragraph,

> As all the living forms of life are the lineal descendants of those which lived long before the Cambrian epoch, we may feel certain that the

ordinary succession by generation has never once
been broken, and that no cataclysm has desolated
the whole world. Hence we may look with some
confidence to a secure future of great length.[14]

In recent years Walter Alvarez and others have produced evidence that Darwin may have been wrong
about the possibility of worldwide cataclysms. It
appears that the extinction of the dinosaurs 65 million years ago may have been caused by a major
impact from an extraterrestrial body, followed by
severe climatic changes. Such changes have been
recently postulated as a result of the use of nuclear
weapons.[15] The danger of producing a "nuclear
winter" is now being seriously studied.[16]

With the explosion of the first atomic bomb on
July 16, 1945, near Alamogordo, New Mexico, the
survival of the human species became a worrisome
issue, although many now realize that survival cannot be assumed even in the absence of nuclear war.
Jonathan Schell emphasized the ecosystem in relation to nuclear war when he wrote in 1982,

> The primary question is not how many people
> would be irradiated, burned, or crushed to death by
> the immediate effects of the bombs but how well
> the ecosphere, regarded as a single living entity, on
> which all forms of life depend for their continued
> existence, would hold up. The issue is the habitabil-
> ity of the earth, and it is in this context, not in the
> context of the direct slaughter of hundreds of mil-
> lions of people by the local effects, that the ques-
> tion of human survival arises."[17]

He noted that

> of all the "modest hopes of human beings," the
> hope that mankind will survive is the most modest,
> since it only brings us to the threshold of all other

> hopes. In entertaining it, we do not yet ask for jus-
> tice, or for freedom, or for happiness, or for any of
> the other things that we may want in life. We do not
> even necessarily ask for our personal survival; we
> ask only that we be *survived*. We ask for assurance
> that when we die as individuals, as we know we
> must, mankind will live on. . . . Life without the
> hope for human survival is a life of despair. (184)

Schell cited Socrates for the principle that the highest good is not life itself—mere survival—but the
moral life (130).

This brings us to the question of what we mean
by survival. Much has been written on the subject,
as seen by book titles alone. We find *Values for
Survival* (Mumford 1946)[18] *Road to Survival* (Vogt
1948)[19] *Science and Survival* (Commoner 1966)[20]
The Crisis of Survival (editors of *The Progressive*
1970)[21] *Exploring New Ethics for Survival* (Hardin
1972)[22] *The Comedy of Survival* (Meeker 1972)[23] *The
Tyranny of Survival* (Callahan 1973)[24] and
Challenge to Survival (Williams 1977).[25] Some of the
issues raised by these authors will be considered
later in this book. But first we must consider what is
meant when the word "survival" is used without
qualification.

In contemplating the term "survival" it should
be pointed out that survival begins today. None of
us knows whether or not we will be alive tomorrow.
On the other hand, the possibility of survival for at
least some members of the human species may
extend into the future for as long as any form of life
exists on the planet. But what kind of survival? We
can think of the kinds of survival that occur in terms
of life-styles and behavior today as well as the kinds
of survival that can be projected into the future. We
can think of the survival of individuals: our children
and grand-children and future generations down

through time. But present behavior and future existence in terms of the kinds of survival I shall describe
applies not only to individuals but also to tribes,
communities, corporations, and governments.
What kinds of survival can be described in the
fewest possible categories?

KINDS OF SURVIVAL

Elsewhere I have proposed that the word "survival," used without a qualifying adjective, is inadequate for discussion in the context of ecological
bioethics. I suggested five categories based on qualifying adjectives: mere, miserable, idealistic, irresponsible, and acceptable.[26]

MERE SURVIVAL

Mere survival is a term used scornfully by
people who dislike talk about survival. Mere survival implies food and shelter but no libraries, no
written history, no engineering, no science, no hospitals, no churches, no television, and, presumably,
no artificial contraceptives: in other words, a hunting and gathering culture, which incidentally is the
only culture that has demonstrated that it can survive for tens of millenia, as in Australia and the Kala-
hari Desert of southern Africa. In the distant past it
may not have been too difficult, but contact with
the white man changed all that.[27]

MISERABLE SURVIVAL

A step below mere survival is miserable survival.
Some millions of Africans on the verge of starvation,
with many actually starving to death, and suffering
from widespread malnutrition, diarrhea, respiratory

disease and parasitic infestations, and now AIDS, provide a ghastly picture of how miserable survival can be much worse than mere survival. Yet both exist today in many parts of the world, and it is a matter of serious debate as to how much the white man's entry into Africa and disruption of the native cultures has contributed to converting mere survival to present-day miserable survival. In their book *Natural Disasters: Acts of God or Acts of Man?*[28] Lloyd Timberlake, editorial director of the London-based group Earthscan, and Anders Wijkman, secretary general of the Swedish Red Cross, said that some disasters, including floods, drought, and famine, are caused more by environmental and resource management than by too much or too little rain, while the effects of natural disasters such as earthquakes, volcanic eruptions, and hurricanes are magnified by unwise human actions. At a press conference in Washington, Timberlake called for refocusing disaster relief which, he said, was often a band-aid on a massive wound.[29] The authors echoed the views of Aldo Leopold in 1933 (see chapter 1) when they said overcultivation, deforestation, and overgrazing tend to reduce the ability of soil to absorb and retain water, making it susceptible to drought and flooding. Population growth and inadequate housing in exposed shantytowns often contribute to larger death tolls from natural disasters, Timberlake said. He noted that in Ethiopia, where famine is threatening millions of people, "the highlands have always been overpopulated and overcultivated."

IDEALISTIC SURVIVAL

At the upper end of the spectrum is idealistic survival. I shall not discuss *ideal* survival because that is something we shall never see, and besides, each person has a private notion of what Utopia would be. However, people can have idealistic survival at many economic levels and in many cultures. Idealistic survival would occur when sufficient numbers of people in a society have the economic security, the information, and the ethical concern to become motivated to think personally about Professor Falk's four planetary dangers, and in particular to think about long-term survival and the amelioration of existing pockets of miserable survival. People cannot agree on the components of ideal survival, but they can universally agree on the undesirability of preventable disease. No culture or religion, primitive or modern, has ever placed a premium on or aspired to starvation, malnutrition, diarrhea, intestinal worms, or other parasitic infestations. So the desirability of eliminating these scourges is something that all can agree upon as a component of idealistic survival.

Smallpox was one of humankind's scourges that decimated populations from time to time, along with typhus, typhoid fever, and many other viral and bacterial infections. But now, international public health efforts have apparently been successful in the total elimination of smallpox from the planet. This was possible because the disease was transmitted from person to person with no intermediate vectors such as mosquitoes, ticks, snails, or other life forms. In the case of smallpox, the last person to have it was prevented from passing it on to anyone else. Idealistic survival would unite people who would seek to eliminate the remaining great miseries that afflict humankind: sexually-transmitted infections, parasitic diseases such as malaria, schistosomiasis and sleeping sickness, intestinal worms of all sorts, and all the other preventable diseases that plague great numbers of the human species.

An example of idealistic survival is the announcement concerning a grant by the MacArthur Foundation for $20 million to fight parasites that cause disease in three billion people around the world. Dr. Jonas Salk, known for his development of a vaccine against polio and now chairman of the foundation's health committee, announced the grant. He said,

> Diseases caused by parasites afflict more than half the world's people. Even when not seriously ill, people who have parasitic disease are chronically sick—weaker, less competent, less productive, and less content than they would be otherwise.[30]

Twelve medical research groups in five states and three foreign nations will participate in the program, which will establish the MacArthur Foundation as the largest private sponsor of parasitology research, according to foundation president John Corbally.

At the same time that we praise the MacArthur Foundation for this example of idealistic survival, we must ask what would be the long-range effects of even partial success of the program on the continent of Africa? Can any program that decreases infant mortality and thereby increases the demands on the ecosystem, without the concomitant educational measures that would protect the ecosystem and promote the idea of zero population growth, be anything but a disaster in the long run? The question is, how bad is a good idea? How can the people of the industrialized nations help the people in the Third World, not with piecemeal efforts or band-aids, as noted by Lloyd Timberlake, but with balanced programs or multi-pronged coordinated programs, when they are unable to control their own unemployment, inflation, environmental pollution, soil erosion, and budget deficits? How can they cope with the dilemma posed by Norman Berrill "that always the more fertile or the more prolific human strains or races will outbreed the rest, that population control by any group sooner or later seals its own doom, with those who retain an uncontrollable breeding instinct taking its place"? The only answer provided by an idealistic survivalist would seem to be that the dissemination of information and motivation for population control, along with public health measures and policies emulating the ethics of Aldo Leopold, is the only sane way to deal with the social dilemma. Both at home and abroad, idealistic survival leads us to Leopold, who said, "An ethic to supplement and guide the economic relation to land presupposes the existence of some mental image of land as a biotic mechanism" (*Almanac*, 214). And at the end of his essay he wrote: "I have purposely presented the land ethic as a product of social evolution . . . I think it is a truism that as the ethical frontier advances from the individual to the community, its intellectual content increases" (225). Idealistic survival surely is an interdisciplinary exercise in democracy. It requires that we listen to the views of both the minority and the majority, and that we try to ascertain the facts. For as Leopold concluded in his essay, "The mechanism of operation is the same for any ethic: social approbation for right actions: social disapproval for wrong actions" (225).

IRRESPONSIBLE SURVIVAL

Irresponsible survival, my fourth category, is in a sense the inverse of idealistic survival. Irresponsible survival is doing all the things that run counter to the aspirations of idealistic survivalists. Whereas proponents of idealistic survival seek to promote

zero or negative population growth for the immediate future and a healthy ecosystem with concern for
future generations, those who are categorized as
irresponsible recognize no obligation to the future,
proceed entirely in terms of self-interest, have no
desire or willingness to control their own reproductive powers or interest in helping others to do so,
and do nothing to preserve a healthy ecosystem. Of
course, there are few who combine all these characteristics. Among the interesting contemporary phe-
nomena are the organizations that are desperately
trying to preserve a healthy ecosystem in terms of
beaches, tidal basins, wilderness, wildlife preserves,
redwood forests, groundwater, clean air, or other
elements in the environment, while ignoring the
fact that it is population pressure that underlies all
of these problems. A sense of ecological morality
will always retreat in the face of economic demands
brought about by the growth of local and world
populations.

As noted earlier in general terms, irresponsible
survival can be discussed in terms of individuals,
local communities, corporations, or governments. It
can be discussed in terms of agriculture, industry,
science and technology, medicine, the military complex, or foreign affairs. Examples are too numerous
to be compiled in detail. In the field of agriculture it
is irresponsible to use farming practices that acceler-
ate soil erosion, or to use deep-well pumping techniques that progressively lower the water table.
According to the 1983 U.S. Geological Survey's
National Water Summary, the combined agricultural, industrial, and residential usage exceeds the
rate of replenishment in thirty-five of the forty-eight
contiguous states.[31] In particular, the states in the
Southwest, whose population increased 6–12 percent as a group between 1980 and 1983, have thirty-
one percent of U.S. water usage but only 6 percent

of the nation's renewable water supply. Water is being "mined" by deeper and deeper wells that must eventually fail to keep pace with demand. State and federal governments are being pressured to implement large-scale projects to import water from somewhere to meet the increased demand caused by population growth. As Leopold said, "Violence (to the land) varies with human population density; a dense population requires a more violent conversion" (see chapter 1).

In the case of chemical herbicides and pesticides applied to the soil, the kinds and quantities produced in ever-increasing amounts exceed the ability of the Environmental Protection Agency to keep abreast of practices. The problems caused by the avalanche of new products and product combinations have resulted in a vast increase in regulatory legislation and a huge bureaucracy faced with an almost superhuman task. That the chemical intermediates and products are basically lethal to many forms of life was dramatically demonstrated on December 3, 1984, in Bhopal, India, when a pesticide intermediate, methyl isocyanate, leaked from a storage tank and killed at least 2,000 residents in the vicinity and injured about 200,000. The justification for the use of toxic chemicals is always a twofold argument—that increased crop yields show a favorable cost/benefit ratio in economic terms, and that increased yields are necessary to feed a hungry and expanding world population.

The Environmental Fund is on record as believing "that every major problem facing the United States as a nation and humanity as a whole becomes more difficult to solve as population increases."[32] Their supporters would have to be classified in the present context as idealistic survivalists, pursuing the twin goals of a healthy ecosystem and a stabilized healthy population with a balance between births and deaths. Their position, supported by many Catholics as well as by non-Catholics, would appear to be on a collision course with the repeated admonitions of Pope John Paul II against artificial contraception and sterilization which, the pontiff said, are "always seriously illicit."[33] In the opinion of many, the Pope would appear to be advocating a course irrevocably committed to irresponsible and, indeed, miserable survival, in terms of net results.[34] Only by continued dialogue between religious leaders and dedicated idealistic survivalists, and between medical ethicists and ecological bioethicists, can some kind of agreement on priorities be reached.

Another example of seemingly irresponsible behavior with respect to future generations and of the effect of economic pressure on priorities is the case of the tobacco industry. The American Cancer Society has for some years pointed to the connection between cigarette smoking and lung cancer. Recently they have publicized dangers to the offspring of mothers who smoke during pregnancy. Cigarette smoking has been credited with causing 30 percent of the total cancer incidence in America. Now the National Advisory Council on Drug Abuse has in effect said that it is irresponsible to promote the sale of cigarettes by advertising in newspapers, magazines, and billboards, and they have proposed a total ban on such advertising.[35] Cigarette advertising on television broadcasts was banned fourteen years ago. Lloyd Johnston, chairman of the council's subcommittee on prevention, said that cigarettes are the most widely advertised product in America, with the industry spending some $1.5 billion a year on advertising. The Federal Trade Commission has estimated that half of all billboards in America advertise cigarettes. Now the economic losses to the industry and to the advertising media will have to be weighed against the fact that smoking is estimated to kill about 350,000 Americans each year, according to the council.

But of all the forms of irresponsible survival with respect to future generations, ignorance, superstition, and illiteracy are the greatest barriers to a hopeful future for our descendants. It has always been said that our children are the hope of the future; but unless they can read and develop skills and an ethical understanding of the natural world, they cannot develop into or select leaders who can plan for tomorrow's world. Leopold said, "Perhaps the most serious obstacle impeding the evolution of a land ethic is the fact that our educational and economic system is headed away from, rather than toward, an intense consciousness of land."

ACCEPTABLE SURVIVAL

Aldo Leopold was concerned with the concept of "carrying-capacity" of the physical environment for the plants, animals, and humans that occupied a given space. We can judge that he was thinking about survival when he wrote in "The Land Ethic" that "North America has a better chance for permanence than Europe, if she can contrive to limit her density." *Contriving* to limit density may suggest limiting human fertility or total immigration; he did not comment on these matters. But with respect to acceptable survival, it is in *Song of the Gavilan* (*Almanac,* 149–54) that we find his critique of technology and his own idea of the good life:

> One of the facts hewn to by science is that every river needs more people, and all people need more inventions, and hence more science; the good life depends on the indefinite extension of this chain of logic. That the good life on any river may likewise depend on the perception of its music, and the preservation of some music to perceive, is a form of doubt not yet entertained by science. (154)

And it is in the foreword to the *Almanac* that we find the comment

> But wherever the truth may lie, this much is crystal-clear: our bigger-and-better society is now like a hypochondriac, so obsessed with its own economic health as to have lost the capacity to remain healthy. . . . Nothing could be more salutary at this stage than a little healthy contempt for a plethora of material blessings. (ix)

In more recent times Lester R. Brown, president and director of The Worldwatch Institute, Washington, D.C., has done the most to urge thought and action to preserve what we can of the natural world in the interests of acceptable survival, or, in his terms, a "sustainable society." In a series of books and brochures from the institute we find a wealth of well-documented material, all of which is relevant to the concept of acceptable survival, including *Losing Ground: Environmental Stress and World Food Prospects* by Erik P. Eckholm.[36] In a powerful effort entitled *Building a Sustainable Society* (1981),[37] Brown describes "The Shape of a Sustainable Society"—which to me is a first attempt to describe acceptable survival—as well as "The Means of Transition," "The Institutional Challenge," and "Changing Values and Shifting Priorities." Summing up the present situation, he said, "We have not inherited the earth from our fathers, we are borrowing it from our children" (359). It is interesting to note that although he seems unfamiliar with Aldo Leopold, he speaks like a true disciple when he comments, "A world that now has over four billion human inhabitants desperately needs a land ethic, a new reverence for land, and a better understanding of the need to use carefully a resource that is too often taken for granted" (352).

1. Norman J. Berrill, *Man's Emerging Mind* (New York: Dodd, Mead and Co., 1955).
2. Alan Gregg, "A Medical Aspect of the Population Problem," *Science* 121 (1955): 681–82.
3. Leopold, *Sand County Almanac,* 1987 ed., 216. The page references herein are from the 1987 edition (see chapter 1, n. 1).
4. Garrett Hardin, "The Tragedy of the Commons," *Science* 162 (1968): 1243–48. This essay has been reprinted in countless subsequent publications.
5. Garrett Hardin, *Exploring New Ethics for Survival* (New York: The Viking Press, 1972; reprint ed., Baltimore: Penguin Books, 1973).
6. Eugene P. Odum and H. T. Odum, *Fundamentals of Ecology,* 3d ed. (Philadelphia: Saunders, 1971), 10.
7. Eugene P. Odum, "Environmental Ethic and Attitude Revolution," in *Philosophy and Environmental Crisis,* ed. Wm. T. Blackstone (Athens: University of Georgia Press, 1974), 14. In this article Odum quoted from Leopold's "Land Ethic."
8. Eugene P. Odum, "The Emergence of Ecology as a New Integrative Discipline," *Science* 195 (1977): 1289–93.
9. Alex B. Novikoff, "The Concept of Integrative Levels and Biology," *Science* 101 (1945): 209–15.
10. Richard Falk, *This Endangered Planet: Prospects and Proposals for Human Survival* (New York: Vintage Books, Random House, 1971), 187.
11. V. R. Potter et al., "Purpose and Function of the University," *Science* 167 (1970): 1590–93.
12. V. R. Potter, *Bioethics, Bridge to the Future* (Englewood Cliffs, N.J.: Prentice-Hall, Inc., 1971), 1–3.
13. J. E. Trosko, "Scientific Views of Human Nature: Implications for the Ethics of Technological Intervention," in *The Culture of Biomedicine,* vol. 1, *Studies in Science and Culture,* ed. D. H. Brock (Cranbury, N.J.: Association of University Presses, Inc.), 70–97.

14. Charles Darwin, *The Origin of Species,* 6th ed. (London: John Murray, 1872), 428.

15. W. Alvarez et al., "The End of the Cretaceous: Sharp Boundary or Gradual Transition," *Science* 223 (1984): 1183–85. See also W. Alvarez et al., "Impact Theory of Mass Extinctions and the Invertebrate Fossil Record," *Science* 223 (1984): 1135–41.

16. R. P. Turco et al., "Nuclear Winter: Global Consequences of Multiple Nuclear Explosions," *Science* 222 (1983): 1283–92. See also P. R. Ehrlich et al., "Long-Term Biological Consequences of Nuclear War," *Science* 222 (1983): 1293–1300.

17. Jonathan Schell, *The Fate of the Earth* (New York: Knopf, 1982), 21, 130, 184.

18. Lewis Mumford, *Values for Survival* (New York: Harcourt, Brace, 1946).

19. Vogt, *Road to Survival.* The author later published *People: Challenge to Survival* (New York: W. Sloane Associates, 1960).

20. Barry Commoner, *Science and Survival* (New York: Viking Press, 1966).

21. *The Progressive, The Crisis of Survival* (Glenview, Ill.: Scott, Foresman, 1970).

22. Garrett Hardin, *Exploring New Ethics for Survival*, (NY Viking Press, 1972), 75.

23. Joseph W. Meeker, *The Comedy of Survival* (New York: Charles Scribners Sons, 1972).

24. Daniel Callahan, *The Tyranny of Survival* (New York: Macmillan, 1973).

25. Leonard Williams, *Challenge to Survival* (New York: Harper Colophon Books, Harper and Row, 1977).

26. V. R. Potter, "Bioethics and the Human Prospect," in *Studies in Science and Culture,* vol. 1, *The Culture of Biomedicine,* ed. D. H. Brock (Cranbury, N.J.: Association of University Presses, Inc., 1984), 124–37.

27. John Yellen, "Bushmen," *Science 85*, May 1985, 40–48. Dr. Yellen is director of the anthropology program at the National Science Foundation.

28. Lloyd Timberlake and Anders Wijkman, *Natural Disasters: Acts of God or Acts of Man* (Washington, D.C.: Earthscan, 1984).

29. "Natural Disasters Said Man-Made," *Wisconsin State Journal,* 15 November 1984.

30. *Wisconsin State Journal,* 17 October 1984. Dr. Jonas Salk was quoted.

31. The Environmental Fund, "Water Availability and Population Growth," TEF Data, No. 16, October 1984. The report was based on data from the U.S. Geological Survey, *National Water Summary* (1983), 26–27; and Bureau of the Census, *Estimates of the Population of the States,* July 1, 1981 to 1983, 2.

32. Stated on most literature from The Environmental Fund, e.g., TEF Data No. 16, October 1984, cited in n. 31.

33. AP, *New York Times; Wisconsin State Journal*, 27 January 1985. Dispatch from Caracas, Venezuela, 27 January 1985.

34. Lester Brown, *Building a Sustainable Society* (New York: W. W. Norton, 1981), 330. Brown commented, "As for population issues, few religious organizations have been at the forefront of social activism and some— among them the Catholic Church and the more fundamentalist Muslim sects—can only be counted as deterrents to progress."

35. National Advisory Council on Drug Abuse, reported in *Wisconsin State Journal,* 27 January 1985.

36. Erik P. Eckholm, *Losing Ground: Environmental Stress and World Food Prospects* (New York: W. W. Norton, 1976).

37. Brown, *Building a Sustainable Society.* This book is by far the most authoritative and best documented with respect to the many issues involved in population, resources, and human survival in the long term.

3

DILEMMAS IN ECOLOGICAL BIOETHICS

WHEN ALDO LEOPOLD completed his textbook on *Game Management* and began the work that would culminate in possibly his greatest contribution, he drew on his extensive background to produce two axioms that deserve our attention today. First, he established a baseline for all future discussions: "An ethic, ecologically, is a limitation on freedom of action in the struggle for existence." Second, he justified his entire arguement for a land ethic on the following basis: "An [ecological] ethic may be regarded as a mode of guidance for meeting ecological situations so new or intricate, or involving such deferred reactions, that the path of social expediency is not discernible to the average individual" (see chapter 1).

The genius of the man was evident in his ability to foresee that there would be situations so new and intricate or with such deferred consequences that exceptional insight would be required to plan in the public interest. He could foresee the dangers in tampering with nature even if he could not imagine the specific dilemmas that today confront governmental agencies charged with the protection of the "average individual." He could not foresee the problems connected with the disposal of the waste products from nuclear power plants or with the disposal of the byproducts of chemical industries. He could not foresee the deliberate dissemination of thousands of tons of pesticides and herbicides on agricultural land. He could not foresee the possibility of a "nuclear winter" that could result from opening exchanges or first-use strikes with nuclear weapons. What he saw was humankind's utter dependence in the long term on the natural environment, which he saw being depleted and degraded even in his own lifetime. What he saw was that drastic changes in the natural environment can destroy its ability to support the human enterprise. He maintained that violence to the natural environment varies with human population density. "A dense population requires a more violent conversion." Thus Leopold was the forerunner of the so-called modern prophets of doom, who proclaim that the human species is on a collision course with disaster *unless* we as a species can make drastic changes in our ethical behavior toward each other, the planet Earth, and its biosphere.

FROM KNOWLEDGE TO WISDOM

The definition of an optimum environment and the value judgments that justify our position constitute the task of ecological bioethics. It is not a task for scientists alone or for humanitists* alone. It is a

---

*The word "humanitist" was not coined by me. Although I have lost the source, the word was coined to refer to people whose disciplines are in one of the humanities. Humanist is often used to describe "humanitists," and to exclude scientists. Humanism is defined as any system or mode of thought or action in which human interests predominate.

task for broad-based humanists who can combine biological and other scientific knowledge with knowledge from the humanities and modify or adapt traditional moral principles on the basis of Leopold's two basic axioms, listed earlier. In 1971 I outlined seven properties that might be found in an optimum environment.[1] These were seen favorably by George H. Kieffer, who reproduced them in his 1979 book, with an extended discussion of "Future Ethics."[2]

When we think of environment we quickly come to realize that the environment in which we live today is largely determined by the culture of the locality into which we are born. The natural features of our environment may seem relatively unimportant to Leopold's "average individual," especially if born and brought to maturity in an urban milieu. However, for those who think about the future, consideration of the role of the natural environment cannot be avoided. Understanding the "is" of the natural environment leads to value judgments of the "ought" for the human species, that is, to an ecological bioethic. As concerned humans we "ought" to consider the "is" of earth's carrying capacity and how it can be enhanced and preserved.

My definition of an optimum environment went beyond the natural environment and inevitably included some aspects of the cultural environment. However, it can be emphasized that medical knowledge, including that of my own background—physiology, nutrition, and cancer research—provides a fairly good consensus on what constitutes normal function as opposed to pathological aberrations. As such we can regard my first two points as basically a description of "what is." It was proposed that an optimum environment:

1. Should provide basic needs that can be satisfied by effort: food, shelter, clothing, space, privacy, leisure, and education (both moral and intellectual).
2. Should provide freedom from toxic chemicals, unnecessary trauma, and preventable disease. Trauma includes unintended exposure to damaging radiation. (Potter, *Bioethics,* 133–48)

This is not the occasion to present in detail all of the current dilemmas in ecological bioethics, but it is clear that bioethical problems are arising from our inability to stem the flood of new hazards, to dispose of them safely, and to heal the biological damage once set in motion. We are presently losing our ability to maintain an environment that is healthful for the human population worldwide, and we are producing many environments that can no longer be considered healthy in terms of the plants, animals, and humans that must reproduce and develop in a nontoxic environment.

THE DOLLAR DILEMMA

DEPLETION & DEGRADATION OF WATER RESOURCES

Wherever we look, we see a shocking disregard for the future water supply. Marc Reisner has documented in detail the depletion of water supplies, while Samuel Epstein, Lester Brown (mentioned earlier), and Carl Pope have dealt with the degradation of the water supply by contamination with hazardous wastes, herbicides, and pesticides.

In his book, *Cadillac Desert,*[3] Reisner discusses the two major ways by which American cities and American agriculture obtain water. The first is by the erection of dams and reservoirs with diversion of the water to wherever it is needed for domestic or industrial use or for irrigation. The second is by pumping water out of the ground from a water-bearing stratum called an aquifer in what is essentially a mining operation, since the water is pumped out at rates far exceeding replenishment by natural rainfall. Pumping groundwater did not begin to approach calamitous rates until the invention of the centrifugal pump shortly after World War I. Either by building dams or by pumping from a subterranean aquifer, the decisions were always based on the dollar dilemma—whether to consider the present or the future. As Reisner states, "In the West, it is said, water flows uphill toward money" (to Los Angeles, Phoenix and Palm Springs) (13). Reisner documents the chronology and history of dam-building in the West, noting the parallel activities and competition by the Bureau of Reclamation and the U.S. Army Corps of Engineers in a highly critical way. He notes that as immediate solutions prove inadequate, proposals become more and more fantastic.

> In the San Joaquin Valley, pumping now exceeds natural replenishment by more than half a trillion gallons a year . . . it is one reason you hear talk about redirecting the Eel and the Klamath and the Columbia and, someday, the Yukon River. (10)

(A proposal released in the early 1960s, called the North American Water and Power Alliance or NAWPA, would divert water from the Canadian Yukon and Tanana rivers 2,000 miles to the American Southwest.)

> The vanishing groundwater in Texas, Kansas, Colorado, Oklahoma, New Mexico, and Nebraska is all part of the Ogalalla Aquifer, which holds two distinctions: one of being the largest discrete aquifer in

> the world, the other of being the fastest disappear-
> ing aquifer in the world. . . . The states knew the
> groundwater couldn't last forever (even if the
> farmers thought it would), so, like the Saudis with
> their oil, they had to decide how long to make it
> last. A reasonable period, they decided, was
> twenty-five to fifty years. (10–11)
>
> The opportunity for economic stability offered
> by the world's largest aquifer . . . was squandered
> for immediate gain. The only inference one can
> draw is that the states felt confident that when they
> ran out of water, the rest of the country would be
> willing to rescue them. (452)

The dilemmas connected with the use of water
resources concern not only the depletion of readily
available sources but their contamination with hazardous chemicals, according to Epstein, Brown, and
Pope in *Hazardous Waste in America.*[4] Deep aquifers like the Ogalalla contain water that has moved
slowly through the earth since being charged by the
runoff from the disappearing glaciers during the Ice
Ages thousands of years ago. The aquifer constitutes
a source of high quality water uncontaminated by
local hazardous wastes. However, as soon as it is dis-
charged above ground it is vulnerable to all the toxic
products in the vicinity. Moreover, the disposal of
hazardous wastes by "deep-well injection" to
depths of a few hundred to over 10,000 feet at up to
70,000 sites has raised the question as to whether
the aquifers can be confidently protected against
contamination. Since the deep-well injection technique is economically attractive, the number of new
wells is increasing by about 20 percent each year.
"In practice, the security of deep-well disposal has
proven illusory" (327).

While some drinking water in metropolitan
areas comes from deep and uncontaminated aquifers, rural areas are generally served by groundwater

from shallow wells. Groundwater accounts for almost 50 percent of the nation's public water supplies. Several major cities, such as Memphis and Miami, are entirely dependent on groundwater, and the U.S. Geologic Survey estimates that 95 percent of all rural Americans obtain their drinking water from wells (300).

> The major sources of groundwater contamination include landfills, surface impoundments, mining activities, oil and gas exploration, waste-injection wells, pesticide and fertilizer use, underground storage tanks, and septic tanks. Additional secondary sources of groundwater contamination include agricultural feed lots, road de-icing salts, leaky sewers, spills, land-spreading of wastes, and salt water encroachment. (302)

The dollar dilemma is everywhere apparent; the conflict between present gain and future health is clearly a bioethical problem whose solution demands access to biological knowledge.

HAZARDOUS WASTE FORMATION & DISPOSAL

Senator Albert Gore, Jr. is one of the nation's leaders who recognizes the magnitude of the bioethical problem and of the dollar dilemma. In the foreword to *Hazardous Waste in America,* he summarizes the situation and the need:

> More than 80 billion pounds of toxic waste are dumped in the United States each and every year, and the volume is steadily growing. Moreover, several thousand abandoned sites caused by the indiscriminate actions of past dumpers have already been identified. . . . The economic interest of industries inconvenienced by remedial efforts have often outweighed the public interest when the critical decisions were made.

Yet the problem not only persists, it is growing. For example, since the end of World War II, the production of organic chemicals in the United States has grown from one billion pounds annually to more than 300 billion pounds annually. And of course the volume of chemical waste has grown proportionately. (ix)

Senator Gore sums up his own views in words that are strikingly congruent with Aldo Leopold's views and with the present demand for a global bioethic:

Our growing numbers and our growing mastery of nature's subtle processes are forcing us to *forge a new ethic of "stewardship"—an ethic which insists that we foresee and account for the future consequences of our present actions."* (x, italics added)

In exhorting the leadership to foresee and account for future consequences, the senator is not demanding the impossible. While the future cannot be predicted in detail, it does not require exceptional biological knowledge to know when poison is poison and that certain substances can produce delayed effects like cancer, birth defects, and subtle pathology at remarkably low concentrations. The problem of regulation is complicated by an avalanche each year of new chemicals that the world has never seen in the natural environment. To assume that the human population will evolve physiological adaptation to these burgeoning insults is sheerest folly, and to assume that medical skills will be able to correct every defect is equally mad.

Presenting the issues in much broader terms than embraced by Reisner, Epstein et al, or Senator Gore, are Richard D. Lamm, three-time governor of Colorado, and Michael McCarthy, in a book that arouses all the best instincts of a Leopold disciple. Far more than a parochial plea, *The Angry West, A*

Vulnerable Land and Its Future speaks for all those who live in contact with the natural environment. Although the opening words are pejorative and partly anticipatory, they set the stage for a sweeping set of assertions:

> Energy combines, unleashed by the government, invade the West. Seeking profit, unconcerned with local fears, they ignore social, political, and economic considerations in the process of building. Huge profits accrue to them and flow out. Little is left to the people and their communities.
>
> Boomtowns mushroom across the West's rural face, disfiguring the land. Cedar breaks crumble to strip miners, water fills with toxic waste, mountain valleys fall to tractor roads, and evening sunsets blaze through polluted air.
>
> Ways of life change forever. Values, attitudes, customs—the core of western life—shatter. New cities, plagued by crime and violence and nonexistent social and economic services, cannot deal with the change.[5]

After describing a winter landscape in words reminiscent of Leopold's *Sand County Almanac,* Lamm and McCarthy conclude as Leopold might have:

> Even in winter, on a day like this, the land is filled with life. On the land, life begins. Here it is lived, and here, too, it ends. The land. It is the sum total of all the West is or ever was.
>
> If it is lost, it is lost forever . . . the dark riders are at the gates. (324)

None of the previous writers cited in this chapter have dealt with a problem that goes beyond local concerns. Air-borne pollution that falls to earth hundreds of miles from its source has commonly been referred to as "acid-rain." The U.S. Congress Office of Technology emphasizes the dollar dilemma: "Our Nation's laws and policies must strike a balance between the economic benefits and environmental risks of fossil fuel combustion and other pollution-producing activities."[6] Sandra Postel has described extensive damage in Germany's Black Forest and in other forests in Europe and the United States.[7] L. B. Parker has described how the emissions from power plants burning fossil fuel can be controlled.[8] Bibliographies like the one by Stopp[9] are available which cover the hundreds of publications on the subject.

Everything that has been said about dilemmas in ecological bioethics was synthesized and extrapolated by Governor Richard Lamm of Colorado in his 1985 book *Megatraumas: America at the Year 2000,*[10] a startling vision of where we might be in the year 2000 unless drastic changes in government policies are made. Nor does he neglect the dilemmas in medical bioethics. Few authors, other than the present effort, have covered the combined issues of medical bioethics and ecological bioethics in a single literary effort, but Lamm does it with imagination and with documentation. Building on the anger of *The Angry West,* he goes on to challenge the status quo of the whole world. As John Baden once said, "We're traveling on the Titanic and all we do is argue about how to place the deck chairs."[11] Lamm describes dilemma after dilemma in both medical and ecological areas. He wrote not to predict what inevitably must be but as a warning of what might be, and based it on much of what is. In words remindful of Aldo Leopold, he commented, "The greatest misperception that Western man has ever entertained is that he is separate from nature and that he can control and exploit it for his material well-being. Human dominion over the earth means all living things will inevitably end in tragedy" (150). Here he clearly means *dominion* with *hubris* and without humility. In his epilogue he reminds us that

> The United States is full of politicians who hide the truth from the public and often from themselves. We break the rules of history, economics, and the social sciences and hope that, for the first time in history, we shall not have to pay the price . . . It is my prayer that someone is listening. (244–45)

Daniel E. Koshland, Jr., a member of the National Academy of Sciences and presently editor of the official AAAS journal, *Science,* commented in a recent editorial on "Inexorable Laws and the Ecosystem":

> With the problem outlined in global terms, it is clear that a rethinking of priorities is necessary. The population explosion has to move to top priority. There is no way that the problems from cars, chemicals, bad land use, and so on, will not accelerate if the population keeps increasing . . . Perhaps the politically feasible line is a negotiated equality of sacrifice. . . . It is time to take a global look at the policies and priorities that are dooming our ecosystem.[12]

Pope John Paul II, in a remarkable encyclical letter entitled "The Social Concerns of the Church," took almost exactly the same view that Koshland expressed, with one exception: he seemed totally oblivious to any problem arising from the exponential increase in human populations. Commenting on the dangers of overconsumption, he stated:

> A naive mechanistic optimism has been replaced by a well-founded anxiety for the fate of humanity.
> At the same time, however, the "economic" concept itself, linked to the word development, has entered into crisis. In fact, there is a better understanding today that the mere accumulation of goods and services, even for the benefit of the majority, is not enough for the realization of human happiness. . . . Unless all the considerable body of resources at man's disposal is guided by an orientation toward the true good of the human race, it easily turns against man to oppress him. . . .

> We find ourselves up against a form of superdeve-
> lopment . . . which consists in an excessive availabil-
> ity of every kind of material goods for the benefit of
> certain social groups. [It] easily makes people slaves
> of "possession" and of immediate gratification, with
> no other horizon than the multiplication of the
> things already owned with others still better. . . . A
> true concept of development cannot ignore the use
> of the elements of nature, the renewability of
> resources and the consequences of haphazard
> industrialization—three considerations which alert
> our consciences to the moral dimensions of
> development.[13]

While Pope John Paul is moving in the direction of a global bioethic, he fails to recognize that there are nonrenewable resources, that the continuing renewability of others cannot be assumed, and finally, that the human capacity to reproduce is at present as much out of control as are the processes of "superdevelopment."[14] When Leopold spoke of the far-reaching effects of man-made changes and of "violence" to the environment increasing along with the human population, he was plainly concerned with the possibility that the human species, with its vast technological power, might have malignant "effects more comprehensive than is intended or foreseen" which might in time destroy its host, an Earth no longer "Mother."

A synthesis of the views of Koshland and Pope John Paul II seems to call for a global bioethic that can transcend the dichotomies between science and religion. In my opinion, such a synthesis cannot do better than to build on the foundation begun by Aldo Leopold when he articulated "The Land Ethic."

1. Van Rensselaer Potter, "How is an Optimum Environment Defined?" in *Bioethics, Bridge to the Future,* ed. V. R. Potter (Englewood Cliffs, N.J.: Prentice-Hall, Inc., 1971), 133–48.

2. George H. Kieffer, "An Ethic of Nature," in *Bioethics, A Textbook of Issues* (Reading, Mass.: Addison-Wesley, 1979), 370–71; and "Obligations to Future Generations," 345. Kieffer argued that there is a close link between images of the future and ethics. "Ethics deals with the realm of what *ought to be* and this automatically presupposes a picture of the future in a way that contrasts with the present. Ethical decisions are normally conclusions for guiding future actions in terms of future consequences." He noted that no previous ethics had to consider the global condition of human life and the far-off future, much less the fate of the entire species. "Accordingly, another aspect of the future must be an ethic of nature."

3. Marc Reisner, *Cadillac Desert. The American West and Its Disappearing Water* (New York: Viking Penguin Inc., 1986).

4. Samuel S. Epstein, Lester R. Brown, and Carl Pope, *Hazardous Waste in America* (San Francisco: Sierra Club Books, 1982). Hundreds of books, articles, and government reports are conveniently assimilated into 395 pages, a massive appendix of 172 pages, and an incredibly detailed author and subject index.

5. Richard D. Lamm and Michael McCarthy, *The Angry West, A Vulnerable Land and Its Future* (Boston: Houghton Mifflin, 1982), 5.

6. Office of Technology Assessment, "The Policy Dilemma," in *Acid Rain and Transported Air Pollutants: Implications for Public Policy* (Washington, D.C.: U.S. Congress OTA-0-204, 1984), 26–37.

7. Sandra Postel, *Air Pollution, Acid Rain, and the Future of Forests,* Worldwatch Paper No. 58 (Washington, D.C.: Worldwatch Institute, 1984). See also Edwin Kiester, Jr., "Death in the Black Forest," *Smithsonian* 16 (1985): 211–30.

8. L. B. Parker, *Mitigating Acid Rain with Technology* (Washington, D.C.: Government Printing Office, 1983).

9. G. H. Stopp, Jr., *Acid Rain: A Bibliography of Research* (Metuchen, N.J.: Scarecrow Press, 1985).

10. Richard D. Lamm, *Megatraumas: America at the Year 2000* (Boston: Houghton Mifflin, 1985).

11. Attributed to John Baden who made essentially this statement at a lecture in Madison, Wisconsin, but documentation not here secured. The allegorical statement is, however, documented by J. Baden and R. L. Stroup, eds., *Bureaucracy vs Environment: The Environmental Costs of Bureaucratic Governance* (Ann Arbor: The University of Michigan Press, 1981). The editors seek the development of private institutions and remodeling of public institutions to foster efficient and noncoercive stewardship of natural resources.

12. Daniel E. Koshland, "Inexorable Laws and the Ecosystem," *Science* 237 (1988): 9.

13. Pope John Paul II, "Solicitudo Rei Socialis" ("The Social Concerns of the Church"), 19 February 1988. Excerpts reprinted in *New York Times*, 20 February 1988.

14. Nicholas Polunin, ed., "Growth Without Ecodisasters? Proceedings of the Second International Conference on Environmental Future (2nd ICEF) held in Reykjavik, Iceland, 5–11 June 1977." An encyclopedic compendium of 675 pages that surveys the hazards of development in a context of population growth. The Editor's Postscript (p. 650) concluded: "Looking back on the Conference through these proceedings, one retains the abiding impression that man now has the knowledge and means to save his world but still shows inadequate signs of acting in time."

4

TWO KINDS OF
BIOETHICS

It seems worthwhile at this point to note the historical development and ongoing evolution of the global bioethics concept. Aldo Leopold laid the framework for an ecological and population-oriented bioethics of survival in 1949 in his seminal essay "The Land Ethic" as well as in earlier essays. Continuing Leopold's line of thought, in 1970 I coined the term "bioethics" to describe the amalgamation of ethical values and biological facts, and in 1971 published *Bioethics, Bridge to the Future.* This concept of bioethics was formalized in a figure published in 1975, here reproduced as figure 1.

However, an independent movement had begun at Georgetown University which utilized the word "bioethics" and applied it exclusively to medical problems in a newly-created Center for Bioethics. Its director, LeRoy Walters, stated, "Bioethics is the branch of applied ethics which studies practices and developments in the biomedical fields."[1] It was

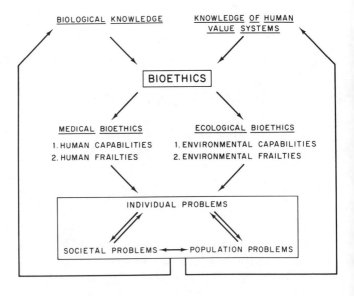

Fig. 1.—Bioethics as a system of morality based on two kinds of knowledge, and its fragmentation into two kinds of applications.

From V. R. Potter, "Humility with Responsibility—A Bioethic for Oncologists: Presidential Address," *Cancer Research* 35 (1975): 2297–2306., with permission of the American Association for Cancer Research.

The two kinds of bioethics are both needed for the solution of the interacting problems shown in the lower box, and attempts to solve these problems lead to new knowledge that feeds back to the original pools of knowledge.

implicit that the focus was on the ethics of individuals in relation to other individuals and not on Aldo Leopold's "third step in a sequence." Evidence for the exclusion of ecological and population problems is abundantly clear from the collection of eighty-seven essays in the 1978 book *Contemporary Issues in Bioethics*, edited by Tom L. Beauchamp of the Kennedy Institute and LeRoy Walters from the Center for Bioethics at Georgetown University. They highlighted their point of view in the preface:

> Recent developments in the biomedical fields have led to considerable moral perplexity about the rights and duties of patients, health professionals, research subjects, and researchers. Since about 1970 . . . members of numerous academic disciplines— including biology, medicine, philosophy, religious studies, and law — have become involved in the complex ethical issues raised by these developments.

Aldo Leopold's land ethic was overlooked as were events such as Earth Day (April 22, 1970), which initiated environmental teach-ins on nearly every campus in the country.

It is not clear why the ethical issues embedded in this entire matter—i.e., the exponential increase in the human population and the impact of this uncontrolled growth on human survival—should not be considered basic to the contributors' discussion of the role of the medical profession in the modern world. Nor is it clear why issues in bioethics should be focused on the moral problems facing the physician who must confront the felt need for performing abortions without discussing the avoidance of pregnancy by means of artificial contraceptives such as condoms (see chapter 5).

More recently, the separate paths taken by medical bioethics and ecological bioethics were noted as shown in figure 2. The further evolution into a global bioethics, as proposed in the present effort, is shown in figure 3. It may be seen that healthy individuals and a healthy environment are given top priority. Controlled human fertility and a world population stabilized at lower levels than seem to be inevitable in the future are considered to be absolute requirements for the twin goals of human health and environmental health.

THE MATTER OF NOMENCLATURE

The general term "bioethics" has to be qualified by mentioning the major areas under discussion. From the outset it has been clear that bioethics must be built on an interdisciplinary or multidisciplinary base. I have proposed two major areas with interests that appear to be separate but which need each other: medical bioethics and ecological bioethics.[2] Medical bioethics and ecological bioethics are non-overlapping in the sense that medical bioethics is chiefly concerned with short-term views: the options open to individuals and their physicians in their attempts to prolong life through the use of organ transplants, artificial organs, experimental chemotherapy, and all the newer developments in the field of medicine. Ecological bioethics clearly has a long-term view that is concerned with what we must do to preserve the ecosystem in a form that is compatible with the continued existence of the human species.[3] However, these two branches of bioethics should properly overlap in the matter of individual human health, the control of human

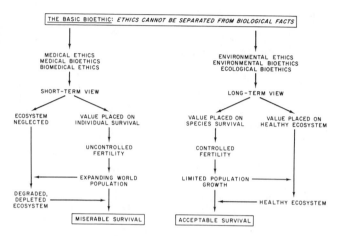

IT'S ALL A MATTER OF BALANCING THE OPTIONS!

Fig. 2.—The hypothetical consequences of the divergent value priorities established by medical ethicists and environmental bioethicists.

It is not intended to imply that the dichotomy is absolute, since individual ethicists will place varying emphases on specific long-term and short-term views. The concept of "acceptable survival" as opposed to "miserable survival" is discussed in chapter 2. Much has been written about environmental ethics without mentioning the need for controlled fertility, while much has been written about the rights of individuals without discussing the need to preserve a healthy ecosystem. In this chart the dual needs for controlled fertility and a healthy ecosystem are seen as essentials for an acceptable survival for the human species. Uncontrolled fertility is seen as the result of an emphasis on individual survival or of death control without an adequate emphasis on birth control by artificial contraception; controlled fertility is not seen as incompatible with individual survival and may in fact enhance it. The chart is intended to emphasize the need for resolving the dichotomy into a unified global bioethics.

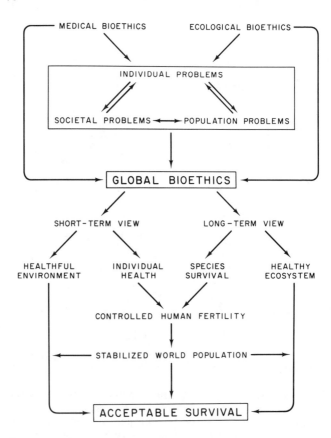

Fig. 3.—Global bioethics as a unification of medical bioethics and ecological bioethics.

The concerns of medical bioethics and ecological bioethics as presented in figure 1 and the short-term vs. long-term dichotomy shown in figure 2 are here resolved into a unified set of goals that include a healthful environment (for people), individual health, species survival, and a healthy ecosystem (as opposed to a degraded and depleted ecosystem as shown in figure 2). With individual health that includes controlled human fertility, the goal of a stabilized world population in a healthful environment, and a healthy ecosystem, it is proposed that global bioethics encompasses a set of values that can lead to acceptable survival for the human species.

reproduction, and in the attitude toward the significance of an ever-expanding human population.*

The drive by professors of philosophy to identify themselves in their new vocations has led to some changes in the labels given the new applications of ethics. Thus, medical bioethics or bioethics has become biomedical ethics.[4] Similarly, professors of philosophy have banded together to form a new journal with the label *Environmental Ethics.*[5] In both of these instances, attention has been given to the professional background in the field of ethics. The early developments at Georgetown University led to the choice of the word bioethics and to the disposal of the long-standing term medical ethics, which could be traced back to the Oath of Hippocrates. Gorovitz decided to refer to medical ethics as dealing with questions of professional etiquette, and he agreed with the evolution of medical ethics into bioethics in conformity with the Georgetown School.[6] In 1986 Gorovitz still employed the term bioethics solely in the medical application.[7]

As described in the preceding chapter, Aldo Leopold used the simplest possible term—land ethic—but then was forced to go to great lengths to explain his meaning: that land is more than soil, more than the space occupied by a shopping center; that land includes water, plants, and animals. For him, land included the whole biosphere. I believe he would go along with the term ecological bioethic, for he repeatedly indicated his emphasis on ecological principles, as when he stated:

---

*Those who regard "overpopulation" as a myth do not even merit citation in my opinion. They include Julian Simon, Ben Wattenberg, and John Tierney. See Robert S. McNamara, "Time Bomb or Myth: The Population Problem," *Foreign Affairs* 62 (1984): 1107–31, for opposition to the myth proponents.

> An ethic, ecologically, is a limitation on freedom of
> action in the struggle for existence. . . . An ethic
> may be regarded as a mode of guidance for meeting
> ecological situations so new or intricate, or involv-
> ing such deferred reactions, that the path of social
> expediency [for humankind's survival] is not dis-
> cernible to the average individual.[8]

I also believe that he would accept the use of the
word bioethics in place of ethics. In his discussion
of the evolution of ethics from interpersonal to the
relation of the individual to society and finally to
"the third step in a sequence," he saw the extension
of ethics to the entire biological community—the
creation of a new ethic not previously enunciated,
in fact an ecological bioethic.

At the present time it is necessary to go beyond
Leopold and beyond medical bioethics. We must
recognize that over-specialization in either branch
can be counterproductive to the goal of acceptable
survival on a global scale. The two branches need to
be harmonized and unified to a consensual point of
view that may well be termed global bioethics,
stressing the two meanings of the word global. A
system of ethics is global, on the one hand, if it is
unified and comprehensive, and in the more usual
sense, if it is worldwide in scope.

THE MATTER OF ETHICS TEACHING
IN HIGHER EDUCATION

According to an unpublished survey of bioethics
teaching by Carola Mone for the Hastings Center,
Clouser estimated that there were over 1500 colleges offering courses in bioethics by 1978.[9] From
an informal survey of college catalogs, Mone found
practically no such courses in existence from 1950
to 1965. In a survey reported in 1977 by Jon
Hendrix,[10] 45 percent of the courses in bioethics

were being taught in biology departments. Biology professors were responding to a popular demand, which was perhaps triggered by the celebration of Earth Day on April 22, 1970. The rise in bioethics teaching in biology departments between 1965 and 1977 also coincides with the many adoptions of my book *Bioethics, Bridge to the Future*.

Clouser explains the narrow views of the medical profession as the inevitable result of the medical school environment:

> The setting is, in fact, a kind of conceptual ghetto, and seems to reflect the setting of all professional schools, not just medicine. When the same presuppositions, purposes, and points of interest are shared by a community, it is as though they are locked into a ghetto. Their view of themselves, others, their relationships, goals and desiderata are the same. (Clouser, 5)

Callahan and Bok have been particularly concerned with the preservation of professional standards in the teaching of ethics in higher education. They comment,

> While a considerable portion of the teaching of ethics takes place within departments of philosophy and religion, taught by those with doctorates in those fields, probably the most significant development in the past decade has been the spread of courses beyond those disciplinary contexts. That spread, in turn, has posed significant questions concerning the qualifications and credentials of those teaching such courses.[11]

They also raise the question of "whether it is possible to teach such courses without engaging in unacceptable indoctrination." On the other hand, William Bennett, former Secretary of Education in the Reagan Administration, has vigorously criticized any unwillingness to assert that some things are right and others wrong that their vision of ethics entails.[12]

THE LIMITS OF PHILOSOPHY

While Callahan and Bok were concerned about the qualifications and credentials of bioethics teachers, Callahan, in another connection, expressed the view that "biomedical ethics must now move into a new phase" because "only rarely can ethical analysis and prescription lead the way in social and cultural change." He noted,

> For some decades, especially during the 40s and 50s, philosophy was a narrow, dry and technical field. Only recently has it come out of its deep slumber, as questions have been raised about the purposes of philosophy. . . . [Thus,] the problems of biomedicine have provided both interesting and difficult material to test the proposition that moral philosophy could, despite its sophisticated detractors, have something to say about human life. In that sense, not only is medicine itself being tested by ethics, but ethics itself is being tested by medicine.[13]

And, we might add, ethics itself is being tested by ecological, population, and pollution crises all over the world.

That the competence of classical philosophy to solve bioethical problems is being questioned cannot be doubted. Bernard Williams, provost of King's College, Cambridge University, himself trained in philosophy, has called for philosophers "to transcend their self-imposed limits and to give full attention to the complexities of the ethical life."[14] Williams is primarily concerned with the *limitations* of philosophy and never approaches the concerns of medical or ecological bioethics. Even in a single case, that of deciding for or against abortion (112–14), Williams does not give a solution but uses the problem to illustrate the difficulties of reason-giving. He states that the attempt to rest the structure of knowledge on some favored class of statements

> has now generally been displaced in favor of a holistic type of model, in which some beliefs can be questioned, justified, or adjusted while others are kept constant, but there is no process by which they can all be questioned at once, or all justified in terms of (almost) nothing. In von Neurath's famous image, we repair the ship while we are on the sea. (113)

A similar commentary on the limitations of philosophy was almost simultaneously published by Professor George Gale of the department of Philosophy, University of Missouri, Kansas City. Gale commented,

> When early twentieth-century physics experienced what can only be called revolutionary upheavals, as the theory of relativity and quantum physics overthrew the classical world view, the classical philosophy developed by Descartes, Leibniz, Newton and Kant was overthrown as well . . . [Thus,] the philosophical consequences of these two new physical theories were at least as important as the theories themselves.[15]

Gale pointed to the growing isolation of philosophy from science in the 40s, 50s, and 60s (cf. Callahan, above), as philosophers were enticed away from the problems of interpreting science in order to focus on problems "internal to the means of interpretation rather than to the substance." Looking toward the future, Gale noted that contemporary biology is a field of increasing interaction between scientists and philosophers. However Gale, like Williams, did not specifically mention the need for applied philosophy in medical or ecological bioethics.

Going beyond the points raised by Callahan, Williams, or Gale regarding the limitations of classical philosophy, Fox and Swazey launched a broad attack against "bioethics" and "bioethicists," terms which they employed in the restricted but widely employed sense that deals only with medical problems.[16] Their objections centered on their conclusion that "it is principally American analytic philosophy—with its emphasis on theory, methodology, and technique, and its utilitarian, Kantian, and 'contractarian' outlooks—in which most of the philosophers who have entered [medical] bioethics were trained" (356). Briefly stated, their objection is that

> individualism is the primary value-complex on which the intellectual and moral edifice of [medical] bioethics rests. Individualism, in this connection, starts with the belief in the importance, uniqueness, dignity, and sovereignty of the individual, and in the sanctity of each individual life. From this flows the assumption that every person is entitled to certain individual rights. Autonomy of self, self-determination, and privacy are regarded as fundamental among these rights. (352)

While the individualism to which they object seems "to reflect and systematically support conventional, relatively conservative American concepts, values, and beliefs" (356), Fox and Swazey are concerned that

> the restricted definition of 'persons as individuals' and of 'persons in relations' that pervades [medical] bioethics makes it difficult to introduce and find an appropriate place for values like decency, kindness, empathy, caring, devotion, service, generosity, altruism, sacrifice, and love.

They object when

> values like these, that center on the bonds between
> self and others and on community, and that include
> both 'strangers' and 'brothers' and future as well as
> present generations in their orbit, are categorized in
> [medical] bioethics as sociological, theological, or
> religious rather than as ethical or moral. (355)

Emphasizing the bipolar choices that the basic individualistic position of (medical) bioethics produces, the authors include "self versus others," "rights versus responsibilities," and "independence versus dependence," among others (355). In a subsequent section I will discuss "responsibility" as a key concept in the proposed global bioethics, and here note that the points made by Fox and Swazey are quite in agreement with my recent characterization of medical bioethics as being primarily concerned with individual survival in a short-term time frame (see Potter, "Response to Clements" Chapter 4, n.3).

The article by Fox and Swazey has not gone unnoticed. In a recent paper entitled "Baiting Bioethics," Gorovitz assembles all the complaints against (medical) bioethics but focuses his rebuttal on Fox and Swazey in particular. He asserts that they have misrepresented some of his own views as part of their case "that individualism and autonomy have an illegitimate hegemony in [medical] bioethical thought." Concluding that "Fox and Swazey have not made their case," he adds, "but despite my criticism of their complaints, I have a lingering sense that their attack on [medical] bioethics would not have been so eloquent or so impassioned were there not a grain of truth in what they say" (Gorovitz, 367).

Clements attacks medical bioethicists from a different angle.[17] She criticizes all those—and Engelhardt[18] in particular—who believe that medical bioethics should be concerned with procedure and the proper functioning of the (medical) bioethical bureaucracy rather than with content.

ETHICS IN A NEW PHASE

In the same vein as Fox and Swazey, Clements and Ciccone, professors of psychiatry at the University of Rochester, specifically and succinctly challenged the philosophic viewpoint as presented by Levine and Lyon-Levine.[19] They noted that these authors assumed that the problem of patient advocacy (the patient's best interest) can best be understood in the classical ethical principles of autonomy and beneficence (medical paternalism), which Clements and Ciccone lumped under the term "universal principles." They expressed the opinion that "most articles on medical ethics routinely reject the inductive method and accept the use of principles" to support the idea, for example, of patient autonomy. They list the arguments and rebuttals as follows:

1. *Moral intuition.* This position states that all of us who aren't "morally depraved" will intuit an autonomy principle. This argument is clearly false if the phrase "morally depraved" isn't included and becomes circular reasoning if it is. What has to be proved has first been assumed; this begs the question. (The shortcomings of reason-giving based on intuition were discussed by Williams, *Limits of Philosophy,* 93–95.)

2. *Faith.* Certain universal ethical principles are part of a belief system. The belief system will work if one accepts the particular theology or faith involved. It must fail for secular ethics.

3. *Democratic procedure.* Within politically created commissions and committees, medical ethicists define the standards for ethical medical practice. [Their proposals confuse] ethics with politics and content with procedure. Medicine in these terms is neither a profession nor a science but a social institution that is driven by social policy.

4. *Choice of universal principles.* It has been suggested that one might be able to choose from a "cafeteria of candidates" for the universal principle—autonomy, beneficence, justice, and equity, among others—based on what makes the ethicist feel intuitively comfortable. [Again, intuition is not enough.][20]

5. *Moral rights.* It is argued that the moral right of autonomy comes from being able to make a valid *claim,* one that is recognized intuitively by everyone as reasonable and valid.

Clements and Ciccone concluded that the attempt to apply universal principles can lead to the installation of taboo systems "validated by the tyranny of numbers or the tyranny of prejudices." They argued that treatment decisions be based on examination of the real world of consequences, the individual situation, and what we know about purpose and functions—in other words, on examination of accumulating experience with similar cases judged against the background of normal development and function (Clements and Ciccone, "Applied Clinical Ethics"). They are in fact calling for a new phase in applied ethics, a new phase that is yet to be enunciated in detail, but which can already be visualized as a methodology for developing a truly global bioethics that embraces the well-being of both the individual and the species.

GLOBAL BIOETHICS AND
THE FEMININE VIEWPOINT

Classical ethics has always been the ethics of individuals, the first two stages mentioned by Aldo Leopold (*Almanac,* 237–64). The emphasis on the ethics of individuals has been clearly male-dominated. Leopold advanced the biologizing of ethics in an ecological framework that emphasized the connections between all forms of life. While he was not thinking in terms of the female role in nature or in society, the current trends in the modern studies on feminine psychology are more congruent with Leopold and ecological bioethics than with classical ethics and current medical bioethics. Indeed, *global bioethics is the logical outcome of the impact of the feminine viewpoint upon medical bioethics and ecological bioethics.* Women who are interested in supporting women's reproductive rights might be expected to support global bioethics as well as birth control, free choice in the matter of abortion, and preservation of a healthy ecosystem.[21] Nearly all will oppose violence, war, and the nuclear armaments race, while many will oppose the domination of political and economic systems by male patterns of thinking.

Carol Gilligan has begun a serious study of psychological theory and its relationship to women's development from childhood to maturity. Her studies are clearly concerned with the concepts developed by ethicists. In reviewing past efforts from Freud to Kohlberg, she stresses again and again how women have been excluded from the critical theory-building studies in psychological research. She builds on the six stages that describe the development of moral judgment from childhood to adulthood as elaborated by Lawrence Kohlberg, but notes that his studies and those of numerous others were based on males. As such, she believes that they are inadequate for present society and are inapplicable to a proper understanding of women's behavior in society. In her view, which I believe can be coupled with Leopold's outlook, *"the moral problem arises from conflicting responsibilities rather than from competing rights" (italics added).*[22] She adds that it

> requires for its resolution a mode of thinking that is contextual and narrative rather than formal and abstract. This conception of morality as concerned with the activity of care centers moral development around the understanding of responsibility and relationships, just as the conception of morality as fairness ties moral development to the understanding of rights and rules. . . . The morality of rights [a male concept] differs from the morality of responsibility in its emphasis on separation rather than connection, in its consideration of the individual [male view] rather than the relationship as primary [female view]." (19)

Agreeing with Miller, [23] Gilligan notes:

> Women not only define themselves in a context of human relationship but also judge themselves in terms of their ability to care. Women's place in man's life cycle has been that of nurturer, caretaker, and helpmate, the weaver of those networks of relationships on which she in turn relies. But while women have thus taken care of men, men have, in their theories of psychological development, as in their economic arrangements, tended to assume or devalue that care. When the focus on individuation and individual achievement extends into adulthood and [when] maturity is equated with personal autonomy, concern with relationships appears as a weakness of women rather than as a human strength. (Gilligan, 17)

In Gilligan's differentiation of women from men, which depicts women as concerned with relationships and care and men as concerned with individuation, individual achievement, and personal autonomy, we can see a parallel with Leopold's reference to the "biotic arrogance of homo americanus." With human ethical theory dominated by males determined to conquer and exploit nature, there has been little chance for Leopold's land ethic to be extended to twenty-first century issues and to include "an intelligent humility toward man's place in nature."[24]

If Gilligan is correct in her analysis of women's ego development as "a function of anatomy and destiny,"* and in her emphasis on the differences in ego development in men and women as partly biological and partly cultural, there may be a basis for hoping that the women's civil rights movement could be recognized as the foundation for a new phase of women's contribution to human progress. Instead of being limited to an Earth Mother fertility image worshipped as an end in itself,[25] the modern woman demands the right to control her own reproductive choices. From that beachhead, women could express a feeling for life and land in the sense envisioned by Aldo Leopold. They could extend the basic female outlook of caring, responsibility, and networking into an outlook that would

---

*I agree with Gilligan: *anatomy* because only women are uniquely equipped to carry, deliver, and breast-feed a child; *destiny* because for many a teenage girl or even an older fertile woman the future includes the possibility that she will face an *unintended* pregnancy, and because human cultures have emphasized that child-bearing is the normal function, while childlessness is unnatural. Small wonder that there may be differences in ego development between men and women!

include the entire ecosystem and humankind, and especially the women and children of the future.

According to Gilligan,

> Whereas the rights conception of morality . . . is geared to arriving at an objectively fair or just resolution to moral dilemmas upon which all rational persons could agree [the universality principle of ethicists], the responsibility conception focuses instead on the limitations of any particular resolution and describes the conflicts that remain. (Gilligan, 21–22; cf. Fox and Swazey)

Here in the responsibility conception we have the basis of a global bioethic, an outlook that would modify the medical emphasis on individual survival and foster peace and ecosystem preservation. The evolution of global bioethics emerges as a development that parallels Gilligan's final comment:

> Through this expansion in perspective, we can begin to envision how a marriage between adult development as it is currently portrayed and women's development as it begins to be seen could lead to a changed understanding of human development and a more generative view of human life. (Gilligan, 174)

The assumption that male and female human development are biologically predestined to be different in their final ethical outlook is not necessary, although this may well be the case. What is important is a further exploration of the insights developed by Gilligan and other professionals who have been led by their study of moral development in girls and women to visualize two models of morality. The "rights" conception of morality, like much of the thought in current medical bioethics, focuses on the individual and can be explored further without necessarily labeling it "male." Similarly, the "responsibility" concept, focusing on relationships, can be developed further without labeling it "female." As foreseen by Leopold, our ethical concepts can be broadened to include his third stage in ethics, in which survival of the species and the survival of a human life-supporting ecosystem is balanced against the "rights" of individuals. Thus, the "responsibility" concept need not be labeled female or embraced by women alone. Indeed, as it is expanded into a global bioethic, the responsibility motif becomes a beachhead for further efforts by both male and female scientists and moral philosophers who hope to promote the welfare and survival of the human species.

The global bioethic must be based on a combination of rights and responsibilities in which masculinity and femininity are no longer viewed as mutually exclusive dimensions of a bipolar continuum. The concept of psychological androgyny, the endorsing of certain traditional attributes of both males and females, and the rejection of certain others, can reorganize traditional perspectives on sex roles.[26]

The greatest barrier to the widespread acceptance of a global bioethic is the "macho" morality of male autonomy and dominance: dominance over women, with unlimited reproductive function in males and confinement of women to the reproductive role; dominance over nature; and conflict with other males. This macho morality is in part the source for the belief that a technological fix can be found for any technological disaster and for the belief that religious Holy Wars are manly. In contrast, perhaps the greatest hope for acceptance of a global bioethic is the women's movement for reproductive freedom, followed by the "changed understanding of human development and a more generative view of human life" as imagined by Gilligan.

1. Tom L. Beauchamp and LeRoy Walters, *Contemporary Issues in Bioethics* (Belmont, Calif.: Wadsworth, 1978). LeRoy Walters discusses "Bioethics as a Field of Ethics," 49–51.

2. V. R. Potter, "Humility with Responsibility—A Bioethic for Oncologists: Presidential Address," *Cancer Research* 35 (1975), 2297–2306.

3. V. R. Potter, "A Response to Clements—Environmental Bioethics: A Call for Controlled Human Fertility in a Healthy Ecosystem," *Perspectives in Biology and Medicine,* 28 (1985): 426–33.

4. Tom L. Beauchamp and James F. Childress, *Principles of Biomedical Ethics* (New York: Oxford University Press, 1979); and James M. Humber and Robert F. Almeder, *Biomedical Ethics and the Law* (New York and London: Plenum Press, 1976).

5. *Environmental Ethics,* 1 (Spring 1979): 1. Defined as "an interdisciplinary journal dedicated to the philosophical aspects of environmental problems." On page 1, the editor comments, "The journal will not have a specific point of view nor will it advocate anything."

6. Samuel Gorovitz, "Bioethics and Social Responsibility," in *Contemporary Issues in Bioethics,* ed. T. L. Beauchamp and L. Walters (Belmont, Calif.: Wadsworth, 1978), 52–60.

7. Samuel Gorovitz, "Baiting Bioethics," *Ethics* 96 (1986): 356–74.

8. Aldo Leopold, "The Land Ethic," in *A Sand County Almanac,* 1987 edition, 202–3. See chap. 1, n. 1.

9. K. Danner Clouser, *The Teaching of Ethics,* vol. 4, *Teaching Bioethics: Strategies, Problems, and Resources* (Hastings-on-Hudson, N.Y.: The Hastings Center, 1980), 48–49.

10. Jon R. Hendrix, "A Survey of Bioethics Courses in U.S. Colleges and Universities," *American Biology Teacher* 39 (February 1977): 85 ff, cited by Clouser, 48.

11. D. Callahan and S. Bok, *Ethics Teaching in Higher Education* (New York: Plenum Press, 1980), xiv-xv.

12. William Bennett, "Getting Ethics," *Commentary* 70 (1980): 62–65.

13. Daniel Callahan, "Shattuck Lecture—Contemporary Biomedical Ethics," *New England Journal of Medicine* 302 (1980): 1228–33.

14. Bernard Williams, *Ethics and the Limits of Philosophy* (Cambridge, Mass.: Harvard University Press, 1985).

15. George Gale, "Science and the Philosophers," *Nature* 112 (6 December 1984): 492–95. Comprehensive, brief and easier to read than Williams' book. Published abstract: "To scientists, the philosophy of science seems an irrelevance, as does the empirical practice of science to philsophers, preoccupied as they are with the logical consistency of their methods. The gulf between the philosophy of science, which has its roots in the growth of positivism in the late nineteenth century, impoverishes both. But there is now hope that the gulf will be bridged by the evolution of philosophy into theory of science."

16. Renee C. Fox and Judith P. Swazey, "Medical Morality is Not Bioethics—Medical Ethics in China and the United States," *Perspectives in Biology and Medicine* 27 (1984): 336–60.

17. C. D. Clements, "The Bureau of Bioethics: Form Without Content is Meaningless," *Perspectives in Biology and Medicine* 27 (1984): 171–82.

18. H. T. Engelhardt, Jr., "Bioethics in Pluralistic Societies," *Perspectives in Biology and Medicine* 26 (1982): 64–78.

19. Colleen D. Clements and J. Richard Ciccone, "Applied Clinical Ethics or Universal Principles," *Hospital and Community Psychiatry* 36 (1985): 121–23; M. L. Levine and M. Lyon-Levine, "Ethical Conflicts at the Interface of Advocacy and Psychiatry," *Hospital and Community Psychiatry* 35 (1984): 665–66.

20. V. R. Potter, "Humility with Responsibility." Intuitions were discussed in connection with "The Eureka Experience," a sudden intuition that cannot be willed or predicted. Experience has shown that an intuition that predicts the outcome of a decision may be correct or incorrect and the incorrect intuition may produce just as much euphoria as a correct one. In ethics as in science, the validity of a prediction can only be tested by experience. However, in the end, although the decisions tailored to each particular case are preferable to bureaucratic dictation of universal principles, such decision will involve reason-giving that falls back on experience in similar cases. But the evaluation of the past experience in ethics as in science will lean heavily on the joint efforts of motivated and qualified participants.

The conclusion that emerges is that a specific decision should be based on ethics that take into consideration a holistic model, and should not be made by one individual in isolation; rather, several individuals should participate, or at least have input in the decision.

21. For example, The American Association of University Women (AAUW) and the National Organization for Women (NOW) are on record as supporting H.R. 700, The Civil Rights Restoration Act, *without anti-choice or other amendments* (see "AAUW, Reproductive Rights: A Tradition of Activism," *Graduate Woman* 80 (1986): 6–7. Cf. Beverly Wildung Harrison, *Our Right to Choose. Toward a New Ethic of Abortion* (Boston: Beacon Press, 1983). An extended discussion of the theme that "the success of present anti-abortion politics would . . . extend the dubious moral reality of female subjugation and male supremacy," 56.

22. Carol Gilligan, *In a Different Voice. Psychological Theory and Women's Development* (Cambridge, Mass.: Harvard University Press, 1982). See also L. Kohlberg, *The Philosophy of Moral Development* (San Francisco: Harper and Row, 1981).

23. Jean Baker Miller, *Toward a New Psychology of Women* (Boston: Beacon Press, 1976).

24. Aldo Leopold, "Why the Wilderness Society?" A 1935 comment reprinted in *Wilderness,* Winter 1984, 22.

25. *Webster's Third New International Dictionary* (Springfield, Mass.: G. C. Merriam Company, 1965). "Earth Mother: The earth viewed (as in primitive theology) as the divine source of terrestrial life; the female principle of fertility." What we need now is a world view in which the sexes can help each other adapt and transcend the restrictive cultural roles of rights and responsibilities that do not allow for full personality development. Men frequently have been able to procreate children while avoiding the responsibility for that choice. Women can now make the choice and can demand shared responsibilities for reproductive choices. Women are saying that fertility is a male/female problem. Fertility should be viewed as a total process of nurturing and paying obligations, or maintaining life's basic processes in a responsible way. Leopold saw this total process as going beyond the microcosm of the individual to the macrocosm of

the entire biosphere. Together men and women can integrate in each the ethics of rights and responsibilities and extend the integration to a global bioethics.

26. V. O. Long, "Relationship of Masculinity to Self-Esteem and Self-Acceptance in Female Professionals, College Students, Clients, and Victims of Domestic Violence," *Journal of Counseling and Clinical Psychology* 54 (1986): 323–27.

5

DILEMMAS IN MEDICAL BIOETHICS

Earlier I proposed that medical bioethicists and medical practitioners are primarily concerned with the short-term view of saving individual lives, with patient autonomy, and with "rights to life." This was seen as frequently in conflict with what I conceived as the ecological bioethic, which pursues the long-term view of acceptable survival for the human species in a healthful biosphere as its goal. In the present chapter I will mention some of the problems that confront medical bioethics and society when life takes precedence over health. The issue is whether "sanctity of life" takes priority over "meaningful life." Ecological bioethics can help the field of medicine in promoting community and societal health, emphasizing responsibilities more than rights.

The field of medical bioethics cannot be looked upon to provide a set of guidelines for the medical profession. Just as the practitioner is faced with dilemmas on every hand and at a time when help is most sorely needed, the sources of help are unable to agree on what to do. In the end, economics may tell the physician whether or not he is permitted to do all that technological advances might permit him to do.[1] Meanwhile, the ethical turf is in dispute and the atmosphere is one of crisis.[2]

On the one hand, the secular ethicists approach medical dilemmas with the classical philosophical search for universal rules, while on the other the religiously oriented rule-givers take the position that all the rules have already been laid down. New-comers to the field are the biologists and clinicians, who may have either a secular or a religious orientation.[3] All who express opinions are likely to have a cryptic bias that reflects their religious upbringing and practices or lack thereof. For ethicists to exclude available knowledge regarding the structure and function of human beings and other living organisms in the biosphere[4] would be as inappropriate as the presently-occurring exclusion of the available facts on Darwinian evolution from the biology courses taught in many of our high schools and some of our colleges. The creationist point of view with its unchanging blueprint for eternity seems a poor foundation for solving the interacting bioethical problems in either health care delivery or biosphere protection. Leopold's land ethic suggests that the human species is responsible for the preservation of the natural environment and for holding the human population within the carrying capacity of the planet Earth.

TEENAGE PREGNANCY

A recent publication opened with a statement that the environmental problems of technocratic-industrial societies are beginning to be seen as manifestations of a continuing environmental crisis that is coming to be understood as a crisis of character and of culture. To meet this crisis, the authors offer an extended exposition of the new term "deep ecology."[5] However, in presenting the dominant world view and the deep ecology alternative (69), the authors fail to mention individual male autonomy to reproduce without responsibility and without societal restrictions. For the deep ecology alternative to omit mention of the need for the prevention of unwanted pregnancies and unwanted births, with all the underlying issues of abortion and teenage pregnancy, seems almost hypocritical.

The matter of teenage pregnancy is an example of a problem that by almost any criterion that might be applied, has reached crisis proportions. But it is a problem that all too frequently is examined in isolation. What is needed is a panoramic perspective that seeks to address the directly related issues of abortion, selective nontreatment of handicapped newborns, the use of cigarettes, drugs, and alcohol by pregnant teenagers (and women), causes and consequences of premature birth, the use of Neonatal Intensive Care Units (NICUs), and the provisions of the various welfare laws along with interpretations of the impact of these laws. The ethical dilemma, stated in starkest terms, is whether to promote or forbid abortions, in particular for teenagers. A case-by-case approach seems called for. The problem is even more complicated than the head-to-head confrontation between so-called pro-life (or anti-choice) and pro-choice factions. For adult women twenty years of age or older, pro-choice is presently a matter of informed decision. But can a fifteen-year-old adolescent caught in an unintended pregnancy make an informed decision under the circumstances which usually accompany such cases? How can the larger society help teenagers to avoid

the need for an abortion or make an informed decision once pregnancy has occurred when the society
is torn between opposing views?

THE NUMBERS

For raw data on teenage pregnancy, the 397-page
*Report of The Select Committee on Children, Youth
and Families* is a useful compendium.[6] The committee concluded, "There is no focused approach to
solving the complex problems of teen pregnancy at
any level of government. The efforts that do exist
are too few, [are] uncoordinated, and lack significant
support. In short, the system is broken" (ix).

The current situation for the United States on an
annual basis (1982) is reported in round numbers for
10.4 million adolescents ages fifteen to nineteen:
over one million teenage pregnancies resulted in
400,000 abortions, over 100,000 miscarriages, and
500,000 births. Fifty-five percent of these births are
to unmarried teens, whose infants are at far greater
risk of low birth weight, and therefore infant mortality. (Details regarding premature births, birth
defects, and mental retardation appear to be unavail-
able.) The births to teens accounted for almost 14
percent of all births, and "most teenage pregnancies
in the United States are unintended" (2). But, significantly, one-third of teenage mothers will have a second pregnancy while still in their teens (2). While
the pregnancy rate increased between 1970 and
1983, the actual number of births and the birth rate
declined due to the increased rate of abortions (3,
20 [fig. 1]). Meanwhile, the percentage of teenage
mothers who were unmarried rose: from 1960 to
1983 the number of unmarried teens giving birth
rose from 15 percent to 54 percent. Births to unmarried teens accounted for nearly 40 percent of all

births to unmarried women (4). The data do not show how many of the "unmarried women" were unmarried teen mothers when their first child was born. Debate as to the role played by legislative assistance to unwed mothers continues.

Birth rates vary for white and minority teens. The rate is much higher for black adolescents (95.5 per 1000 in 1983) than for white adolescents (43.6 per 1000 in 1983). "Black adolescents also begin childbearing at younger ages than whites, increasing the likelihood of subsequent births during the teenage years" (4, 23 [Table 2]). But the correlation is with poverty: "Families headed by young mothers are seven times more likely to be living below the poverty level than other families" (14).

"Children of teen parents tend to be less healthy on the average than other children, and to exhibit learning difficulties more frequently in school. They also are likely to become teen parents themselves" (17). "Low birth weight, which is strongly associated with infant mortality, remains high among infants born to teens. Teenage mothers typically account for about 1 in 5 low birthweight infants. In 1983, there were 47,500 low birthweight infants born to teens under 20, almost 20 percent of all births to teens" (12). These facts may suggest that the adoption of a teenager's offspring may involve a risk. Data show that in 1971, 2 percent of unmarried black teenagers and 18 percent of unmarried white teenagers who gave birth placed their children for adoption. By 1976 the figure for whites had dropped to 7 percent and the black rate had dropped to zero. Again, the availability of welfare may have affected the number of infants offered for adoption.

The impact of low birth weight on medical bioethics has been reflected in a recent article by Hack and Fanaroff.[7] In the report, 98 infants born at a gestational age of twenty to thirty weeks had birth weights between 260 and 740 grams. Twenty infants survived but all required active respiratory support, prolonged intensive care, and hospitalization. The developmental outcome reflects a handicap rate approaching one-third of all survivors. "When weighing the final outcome, the enormous ongoing medical, financial, and social costs must be considered. . . . The poor previous reproductive history of the majority of the mothers . . . indicates a need for preventing or treating the causes of the immature births, rather than expending resources on prolonged neonatal intensive care. The implications and cost-benefit ratios of extending the trend whereby intensive care is applied to progressively smaller immature infants must be seriously considered *in order for definitive guidelines to be devised*" (italics added). The authors did not comment on the number of teenage mothers in the group of 90 mothers, but 52 were unmarried. Since the number of unmarried teenage mothers is increasing and since their infants are frequently underweight, the lack of ethical guidelines for treating premature infants is certainly part of the teenage pregnancy issue.

THE INCREASE IN ONE-PARENT FAMILIES

It was noted above that the number of unmarried teen mothers has increased rapidly and that births to unmarried teens accounted for 40 percent of all births to unmarried women. But how many of the post-teen unmarried mothers began childbearing as unmarried teenagers? The share of births to single parents that is attributable to teenage pregnancy may actually be much greater than 40 percent. Senator Daniel Moynihan has been especially cognizant of the impact of the increasing number of single-parent families on society, in terms of school performance, poverty, and crime. In his book *Family and Nation*[8] he cites alarming findings. In one study school performance was reported: among all two-parent children, 30 percent were ranked as high achievers, compared to only 1 percent of one-parent children. At the low end, only 2 percent of two-parent children were low achievers while 40 percent of one-parent children fell in that category (92–93). As for poverty, in 1984 there were 33,700,000 Americans living below the poverty line. Of these, 16,440,000 lived in female-headed families (96). Moynihan implied that the home life of children of unprepared teenage mothers in female-headed households is likely to have "features that make for criminality" (98). Looking to the future, it was projected that in the period 1980–2000, the number of female-headed families will increase at more than five times the rate of husband-wife families (147). Whatever the effects of teenage pregnancy and female-headed families—and none appear to be favorable—the phenomenon is on the increase.

THE ABORTION ISSUE

The matter of abortion may be examined in several ways. First, what are the facts, and second, what are the consequences under present conditions or in the future if the percentages increase or decrease? Moynihan reports succinctly that each year 60 of every 1000 American women under age eighteen have abortions. In Canada the rate is 18 per 1000, and in The Netherlands only 7 of every 1000. Put another way, fully 40 percent of all pregnancies in American teenagers end in abortion (171). What would be the consequences if the practice were encouraged to approach 100 percent? We know that making the practice illegal would not reduce the figure to zero percent.

This is an issue that has aroused more ethical disagreement than any other in recent times. The goal of preserving the two-parent family and increasing the quality and financial independence of the children who will become the citizens of the future is at stake. The issue is one in which secular ethicists, biologists, and clinicians are confronted by the New Right coalitions of religious conservatives who oppose abortion categorically. Moynihan quoted the obvious when he cited the *New York Times:* "Teenagers need help to avoid pregnancy, and to avoid abortion." He then asked "Should not there be a national effort to protect children from both?" He noted that in New York City in 1983, 1,292 girls under the age of fifteen became pregnant, followed by abortions for 988 (172–73). It seems inconceivable that any ethical approach to the problem could advocate an end to abortions without agreeing with Moynihan that every effort should be made to help teenagers avoid pregnancy.

Yet this is precisely where the ethical crisis is most poignant. Those who oppose abortion most violently cannot agree on how teenagers should be helped to avoid pregnancy. They tend to oppose sex education and increased availability of contraceptives, the two most likely explanations for the low rate of abortions in The Netherlands. On the other hand, if no help in avoiding pregnancy is given, and if abortion is outlawed, will these policies be willingly coupled with new welfare policies that would help the unmarried teenage mother to complete her education and become employed and able to provide a suitable home for her offspring? Again we turn to Moynihan, who remarks, "The national policies we have affecting pregnant teenagers, and those at risk of becoming so, are filled with contradictions. . . .We subsidize family planning services for teenagers while encouraging them not to seek them" (172). In noting the para- doxes in the AFDC program (Aid For Dependent Children), he notes that there are few solutions that can be put in place as regulations; case-by-case social work is required. In other words, the categor- ical rules of the religious conservative or the univer- sal rules of the secular ethicist are both inadequate, but the case-by-case approach begins to touch "the limits of government."

The thought leads back to the assertion that "a credible family policy will insist that responsibility begins with the individual, then the family, and only then the community" (173). It appears reasonable to suggest that the teenage girl should be acquainted with the available information, and with a degree of parental influence should be permitted to choose from a variety of options, that is, to be responsible for her own decisions (see my chapter 7). With ade- quate pregnancy prevention it might be possible to reduce the number of abortions drastically. With freedom to choose a medically safe, legal abortion, a teenager might suddenly acquire the ability to pre- vent a second pregnancy and might choose to be responsible for postponing pregnancy until she could parent a child with a responsible father. But Moynihan concludes, with Urie Bronfenbrenner, that

> A child requires public policies and practices that provide opportunity, status, example, encourage- ment, stability, and above all, time for parenthood, primarily by parents, but also by all adults in the society. And unless you have those external sup- ports, the internal systems can't work. They fail. (192)

The final conclusion is on the whole despairing, but the one optimistic note seems to be that "the needs of families might be the means for bringing liberals and conservatives together on matters of policy" (188). Meanwhile, the polarization between anti-choice and pro-choice factions appears to be increasing, while the pregnant teenager living in poverty and the conscientious legislator who would like to help are caught in the cross fire.

THE 1985 WISCONSIN LEGISLATION

During 1985 a "Special Committee on Pregnancy Options" was set up by the Wisconsin State Assembly under the chairmanship of Assemblyman Marlin Schneider.[9] The committee included eleven public members who personally held extreme pro-choice or anti-choice/anti-abortion views. Despite the divergence in views, they had some common goals that they were able to address. The title of the act finally passed was the "Abortion Prevention and Family Responsibility Act of 1985." It stated:

> The high number of unintended or unwanted preg-
> nancies and the resultant high number of abortions
> is a tragic and undesirable consequence of complex
> societal problems. Strong efforts must be made to
> ensure that unintended pregnancies do not become
> unwanted pregnancies. . . . It is clear that among
> adolescents the burden of unwanted pregnancies
> presently is borne by the adolescent mothers and
> that ways must be found for adolescent fathers, *as
> well as the parents of adolescents,* to share this
> responsibility (italics added).

What may be a novel aspect of the legislation is that the bill makes grandparents responsible for the support of a child of one of their dependent minor children. Under the bill, the parents of the minor mother would assume such responsibility upon the birth of the child; the parents of the minor father would assume that responsibility only after he has been determined to be the father. Each set of grandparents has an equal responsibility to support the newborn child, but their responsibility ends when their own child reaches age eighteen.

Only future experience will make it possible to determine whether the grandparenting sections of the bill will have the effect of decreasing unintended pregnancies or of increasing the number of abortions. The bill repealed previous state laws restricting the sale of nonprescription contraceptives and a separate bill was subsequently passed permitting the sale of condoms in vending machines. The bill also repealed a Wisconsin criminal law on abortion to conform to the 1973 U.S. Supreme Court decision on abortion.

Since the effect of the law on the attitudes of the parents of adolescents who may become pregnant or who have become pregnant cannot be predicted, the Department of Health and Social Services is mandated by the law to submit by 1 January 1989 a report to the presiding officer of each house of the legislature concerning the impact of the requirements for grandparents' support of children of their minor children.

DILEMMAS IN THE CASE OF HANDICAPPED NEWBORNS

Recent developments in medical technology and instrumentation have occurred in a milieu in which the goal of the medical practitioner has always been the preservation and extension of life in the individual patient. Until recently, physicians have been asked to assume that all life—no matter how miserable, or extended for however brief a time, or at what cost—is preferable to death. Medical practitioners have not individually or collectively sought to pass judgment on the overall consequences of their increased power to aid individuals. On the other hand, the word "dilemma" has appeared everywhere in discussions of the problems raised by the new technologies. In his far-seeing "Shattuck Lecture on Contemporary Biomedical Ethics," Daniel Callahan speaks of "difficult moral dilemmas" and "moral dilemmas generated by emergent technologies."[10] After a thorough analysis of the problems, he concludes that "biomedical ethics must now move into a new phase, one that will force a rethinking of its role, its methodology, and its relation to other disciplines and institutions." My present effort sees this new phase as one in which medical bioethicists must examine, with the help of medical doctors, ecologists, demographers, and others, the significance of Aldo Leopold's land ethic. They must consider how the practice of medicine can evolve guidelines that can lead to societal as well as to individual health and well-being. However, it would be tragic indeed if the practice of medicine came to be dominated by purely political considerations.

As mentioned earlier, the word "dilemma" is the only one that can describe the present situation in many areas of medical practice. The term is especially apt in the case of the NICU—The Neonatal Intensive Care Unit. (A neonate is a newborn infant in its first four weeks of life.) As examples of the usage one may note titles such as "Moral and Ethical Dilemmas in the Special-Care Nursery" by Duff and Campbell,[11] a courageous and incisive report; "Dilemmas of 'Informed Consent' in Children" by Anthony Shaw[12] and "Selective Nontreatment of Handicapped Newborns: Moral Dilemmas in

Neonatal Medicine" by Robert F. Weir.[13] All of these
studies are recommended for in-depth coverage and
will be referred to below. In addition, there is the
outstanding book by Jeff Lyon, *Playing God in the
Nursery*,[14] a title that certainly suggests that dilemmas arise whenever human individuals have to
make decisions to preserve or to end the life of
another.

SELECTIVE NONTREATMENT

Nine years before the "Baby Doe" incident (see
Lyon, 21–58), Duff and Campbell noted that
between 1940 and 1970 there was a 58 percent
decrease in the infant death rate in the United States,
which they attributed to the installation of infant
intensive care units (NICUs). While some survivors
from the NICU may be healthy, others continue to
suffer from such conditions as chronic cardiopul-
monary disease, short-bowel syndrome, or various
manifestations of brain damage; they noted that others are severely handicapped by myriad congenital
malformations that in previous times would have
resulted in early death. Their summary stated,

> Of 299 consecutive deaths occurring in a special-
> care nursery, 43 (14 percent) were related to with-
> holding treatment. In this group were fifteen with
> multiple anomalies, eight with trisomy, eight with
> cardiopulmonary disease, seven with meningomye-
> locele, three with other central-nervous-system dis-
> orders, and two with short-bowel syndrome.

In each case parents and physicians joined in the
decision that "prognosis for meaningful life was
extremely poor or hopeless, and therefore rejected
further treatment." Thus in these forty-three cases
"meaningful life" as a concept took priority over
any other consideration, and in a sense the role of

"playing God" was accepted. Yet the authors were firm in stating, "The issue has to be faced, for not to decide is an arbitrary and potentially devastating decision of default." The authors commented that "many pediatricians and others are distressed with the long-term results of pressing on and on to save life at all costs and in all circumstances." They quoted Eliot Slater approvingly, who said, "If this is one of the consequences of the sanctity-of-life ethic, perhaps our formulation of the principle should be revised."[15] This view was also advanced by M. Harry Jennison, executive director of the American Academy of Pediatrics, in his foreword to Lyon's book: "In spite of modern technology, there are limits to what we ought to feel obliged to impose on dying patients and on those whose futures are overmastered by futility." In a similar vein, Landau and Gustafson, in a commentary titled "Death is Not the Enemy," wrote: "The development of technologies with the prime aim of prolonging life should be seriously questioned if the ultimate result is destined to be a grotesque, fragmented, or inordinately expensive existence."[16] Yet the ultimate result is frequently concealed, and today parents are being pressured to believe that their defective infant is salvageable by medical science.

Robert Weir, a professor of religious studies at Oklahoma State University, surveyed the situation in 1984 not long after the Baby Doe case had captured public attention.[17] His book and that of Lyons supplement each other to a remarkable degree. Both describe the chronology of the legal maneuvers and administrative rulings that followed. More recently it has been reported that federal efforts to lay down hospital rules regarding cases of handicapped infants have been struck down by lower courts and the U.S. Supreme Court.[18] Earlier it was reported that the American Jewish Congress and the Pro-Life

Committee of the National Conference of Catholic Bishops have issued a consensus statement in which they stated, "Handicaps, in and of themselves, do not justify withholding treatment," but intervention is not required when it would be "clearly futile and would do no more than briefly prolong the act of dying."[19] Their position appears to avoid the issue of quality of life. However, if medical experts disagree, the parents are obligated to decide in their child's "best interest." The dilemma remains, but parental discretion appears to be emerging as a key formula.

Weir adopted a comprehensive method of documentation, with a description of handicapped infant syndromes, case histories, legal cases, and historical records of society's views on infanticide which could be regarded as equivalent to or in some cases preferable to withholding treatment. Weir presented the views of seven pediatricians, who included Duff, Shaw (both mentioned earlier), and C. Everett Koop, Surgeon General of the United States. All have different and opposing views and in several cases are critical of each other. Koop reported with pride the case of an infant who went through thirty-seven operations, of which Koop performed twenty-two. Clearly the dilemma for physicians and parents remains.

Weir also surveyed the views of seven attorneys and again, differing and opposing views were held. John Robertson, one of the attorneys, clearly advocated the view that, with few exceptions, the application of criminal liability to withholding care may be "both desirable and morally compelled." For Robertson, even though the wards for retarded children in state institutions are often "an apt description of hell," the termination of parental rights in a custody hearing and assignment of a child to an institution "is not clearly a worse alternative than death" for the child. Weir noted that the federal moves to restrict parental and physician discretion, advocated by Koop, were subject to the criticism that they frequently fail to distinguish between handicaps that can be corrected and those which cannot.

When ethicists were surveyed, divergent views were again highlighted. While some believe in the sanctity of life, no matter what, others, especially Michael Tooley, reject that principle and argue that the morality of abortion and infanticide—including withholding medical treatment—hang on the conceptual issue of "personhood."[20] Engelhardt has taken a similar view.[21] In particular, the plight of parents is considered. The basic view is that withholding treatment or deciding to abort a fetus is primarily a matter of parental discretion.

Weir comments (178) that one of the problems common to the ethical literature is the minimal attention given to the medical realities and the range of cases that actually characterize the NICUs. In addition, there is the vagueness of terminology used by ethicists—for example, the meanings of "sanctity of life," "quality of life," "harm," "meaningful life," "human," and "person."

RESPONSIBILITY MUST BE ACCEPTED

Elsewhere I have argued that the keynote here as in other cases is responsibility.[22] The issue of teenage pregnancy is inextricably interwoven with decisions involving abortion, nontreatment of handicapped newborns, and even infanticide.

The alternatives of choosing abortion, infanticide, or nontreatment for a handicapped newborn are classic examples of the controversies surrounding the concept of nontreatment in the absence of prospects for meaningful life. The present state of affairs seems to encourage nondecisions by both parents and pediatricians. The parents have been encouraged to indulge in nondecisions by laws that require the "maintenance" of defective surviving infants in state-supported facilities if the parents are unable to undertake the burden. What would be the situation if parents were given accurate information about the infant's condition and prospects after "treatment" and were told that its maintenance was their responsibility? What if they were told that for the type of defect at hand, the very next pregnancy would probably yield a normal child? If the parents and the physician shared the responsibility for the decision and the parents had to bear the major responsibility for the outcome, the commonsense delineation of meaningful life would not be delayed for long. Moreover, in the case of many handi-capped newborns, the condition is hereditary. In such cases the parents should be told when their situation is the type that can be readily diagnosed both in the parents and in the fetus *in utero*. They should be told when, despite the occurrence of one homozygous defective fetus or newborn, their chances of a nonsymptomatic newborn infant in the next pregnancy are three out or four. It should be explained that a homozygous *normal* infant may occur in one out of four pregnancies, and that a homozygous *defective* infant may occur a second time, also with a probability of one out of four, in which case they could abort and try again. In such cases, how many parents would elect treatment for a handicapped newborn that they would have to maintain for the rest of their lives, and in addition possibly forego the option of having a normal child? They should be told whether "treatment" would produce a normal child, since in most cases it does not.

Going back to the 1973 report (Duff and Campbell) in which 43 (14 percent) of a total of 299 deaths were due to nontreatment, 256 (86 percent) resulted from pathology that prevailed *despite the treatment given*. Of these, 66 percent were the result of respiratory problems or complications associated with extreme prematurity (birth weight under 1000 g). From the standpoint of applied bioethics, the problem is not the 299 newborns that died but the defective newborns that were treated and survived, escaping any decision to withhold treatment. What kind of survival was given them? While mortality in hospitals that have a NICU is about half that reported for hospitals lacking such units, an unreported number of treated surviving infants are severely handicapped by "a myriad of congenital malformations that in previous times would have resulted in earlier death" (Duff and Campbell). Various manifestations of brain damage also persist. At present these cases can be abandoned by their parents, who may have brought on extreme prematurity or defects by the use of alcohol, cigarettes, or drugs. Would it not be better to put less emphasis on maintaining premature and defective infants in NICUs at fantastic cost, with possible abandonment and miserable survival, and instead stress the knowledge that could bring about a normal birth? Would it not be better to abort a defective fetus than to give birth to a permanently handicapped infant? It is time to reach a consensus on the criteria as to which defects can permit meaningful life at home or in an institution and which cannot.

Just as the legal profession, through malpractice suits, has pushed the medical profession into maximizing the application of life-sustaining technology, the legal experts have lately picked up the opportunity to sue for failure to advise abortion (or to inform the prospective parents of their situation and options). Just as the physician can be sued for failure to treat a handicapped newborn, suit can also be brought for failure to advise a patient of the options involving amniocentesis and possible abortion.[23]

The bottom line, in all of the cases involving issues of meaningful life, is responsibility. Decisions made on behalf of fetuses or newborn infants should be shared by physicians and by parents who have been properly informed as to the biological facts in the individual case. When public facilities are available to relieve parents of the responsibility of maintaining a defective child for life, the parents should be fully informed as to the possibilities for meaningful life for their child in the available institution, where it is widely agreed that life for a severely defective child comes close to "a definition of hell" as noted earlier.[24] Again, the parents should bear the responsibility for their decision or nondecision and should be informed of possible contingencies during prenatal care, while their physician should bear the responsibility for advising them of their present and future options.

ORGAN TRANSPLANTATION

Organ transplantation has been performed in adults for many years, especially in the case of kidney failure, and more recently, in the cases of hearts and livers. Humans have two kidneys and can survive, leading a normal life, with only one kidney. Thus a donor can give one kidney to an appropriate recipient and go on living. Not so in the case of hearts and livers, since of these we have but one. In these cases the adult donors must be victims of automobile accidents or gunshot wounds, which are in plentiful supply in this country. The donors must be incapable of sustaining meaningful life and their permission must be supplied by a responsible parent or spouse. More recently, organ transplants have been carried out in newborns or very young infants, the handicapped newborns who might be subjected to "selective nontreatment" as discussed in the preceding two sections.

TRANSPLANTS INVOLVING HANDICAPPED NEWBORNS

Rapidly advancing medical technology has again forced dilemmas upon medical bioethicists. In previous times a handicapped newborn with fatal pathology in the brain, heart, or liver presented no particular ethical problems. Death would supervene with whatever treatment. In the earliest attempts, treatment by means of organ transplantation from an infant fatally damaged in an automobile accident was attempted and probably undocumented. In the past few years heart and liver transplants in infants have been carried out successfully in a number of hospitals and widely reported in the media. More recently a new possibility has emerged. A handicapped newborn may have fatal pathology in heart, liver, or brain but not in all three. This creates the technological opportunity to salvage a viable organ from one defective newborn and replace the corresponding nonviable organ in a second defective newborn, thus sacrificing (killing?) the brain-dead donor. The choice may be offensive but it is rational, in a limited sense, if the donor has essentially no brain function but a normal heart.[25] Such an infant could be maintained alive with heroic efforts for extended periods but its life would not be "meaningful." Many attorneys, pediatricians, and ethicists have argued, in terms of the "sanctity of life," that such a life cannot be "terminated." But now they are confronted by a new alternative. The brain-deficient newborn can contribute its good heart to a heart-defective newborn who would otherwise surely die. Not only does this alternative exist, but the brain-defective infant could be kept alive until a heart-defective infant came along, or until a liver-defective infant came along, or until the two defective infants became available. What is the ethical decision now? How bad is a good thing? The described dilemma is not theoretical: it recently came to pass in California and was widely reported in the media. A neonate with a severe heart defect was born to an unwed minor. A 16-day-old neonate with a defective brain was used to obtain a viable heart, with permission granted by its parents, whose child was many miles from the planned recipient. The transplant was reported as successful.[26]

TRANSPLANTS INVOLVING ADULTS

The demand for liver transplants is increasing exponentially. Dr. Thomas E. Starzl of the University of Pittsburgh School of Medicine, who pioneered the operation, said that the number at his location increased from 14 in 1980 to an estimated 250 this year.[27] He said that many who could be helped die for lack of a donor liver. To increase the supply of organs he recommended relaxing the requirements as to when a patient is considered brain-dead and available as a donor; removing donor age limits; developing teams in emergency rooms that would be available to remove donor organs from people who are dead on arrival; and changing laws on organ donation to *presumed* consent, meaning doctors would be free to remove organs from a dead person unless he or she objected *beforehand,* thereby creating new ethical problems.

A comprehensive report on the issue of who gets the organ transplants was recently described.[28] The Task Force on Organ Transplantation said the United States should expand access to organ transplants for its own citizens, regardless of their wealth or insurance coverage, but should limit access for aliens who come to this country seeking transplants. They recommended that aliens who come to the United States for surgery should receive no more than 10 percent of the kidney transplants at any hospital. Heart and liver transplants should be reserved for American citizens and permanent residents wherever possible. The panel noted that organs are donated by rich and poor alike but that poor people often cannot afford transplants or maintenance therapy.

Organ transplants are increasing in part because of a new drug, cyclosporin, that suppresses the tendency of the body's immune system to reject foreign organs and tissues. The present cost of treatment is about $500 per month and must be continued for life. The number of kidney transplants rose from 4,886 in 1981 to 7,800 in 1985; heart transplants rose from 62 to 719 and liver transplants rose from 26 to 602 in the same period. The increases were made possible because unmatched donors could be used in conjunction with cyclosporin treatment.

A member of the panel, Roger W. Evans, a medical sociologist at the Battelle Human Affairs Research Centers in Seattle, Washington, estimated the average first-year cost for a kidney transplant at $35,000, for a heart transplant at $95,000, and for a liver transplant at $135,00.

The panel said the selection of transplant patients must be based solely on objective medical criteria such as the patient's need and the probability of a successful transplant. They thus by-passed the ethical dilemma of deciding whether the life of one patient is more important (to society) than the life of another patient, when a choice must be made. The panel condemned the "commercialization of organ transplants" that is now occurring in the case of kidney transplants since, as noted above, a donor can sell one kidney and survive with only one remaining. However, a year-old federal law makes it illegal to buy, sell, or profiteer in human organs for transplant in the United States.

Now that the beating heart of a brain-dead newborn infant has been transplanted to the body of a newborn with hypoplastic left-heart syndrome, one can imagine the possible use of a heart from a hospital patient who has survived without a respirator for months or years in a vegetative state but who is not totally brain-dead, as in the case of Karen Quinlan (Engelhardt, *Foundations,* 211). Such a person contrasts with the victims of automobile accidents or gunshot wounds who may not be capable of sustained existence. But it may be revolting to utilize the heart of a Karen Quinlan, who was once a person, in contrast to the permissible use of the heart of a vegetative-state newborn who in the minds of many people was never a person and never could be.

ARTIFICIAL ORGANS

The alternative to a kidney transplant is artificial dialysis, which can be done in a hospital or under a patient's own management. The numbers and problems will not be documented here, but it is clear that although a meaningful life can still occur, it becomes increasingly burdensome and difficult. Nevertheless, the procedure is widespread.

Completely experimental, and thus far tried in only a few patients, is the plastic pump implanted in the chest as an artificial heart and powered by an external source. I feel that the device overlooks the fact that the heart is much more than a pump. It has a special oxidative metabolism, the details of which differ from all other organs,[29] and in addition produces a special hormone.[30] There seems to be no justification for assuming that this mechanical device could ever replace a human heart.[31] The only justification for continuing its development might be its possible use for a few days until a suitable donor of an actual human heart could be found, but as pointed out earlier in the case of handicapped newborns, the transplantation of human hearts raises new ethical problems.

EUTHANASIA

For centuries people have argued about whether to facilitate the death of a fellow human who wishes to be helped to die or who it is presumed would wish to die if capable of making the decision. Euthanasia, taken literally, means normal death, implying that nature has been let to take its course. Recently it has been taken to mean good or easy death and to mean a "mercy killing," the bringing about of such a death for a person by a friend or family member or by the health care system. In a hospital or nursing home D.N.R. stands for "Do Not Resuscitate"—a label for patients whose lives are not to be saved should respiration or heartbeat fail. The label is surrepticious because of the absence of laws or guidelines that specify when it is legitimate to let nature take over. Thus we see another dilemma for medical bioethics—the need for policy clarification on a subject that brings deeply divided opinions. The

New York State Task Force on Life and the Law recently recommended legislation that would set guidelines for D.N.R. orders.[32] It was proposed that the D.N.R. order would be legal only if the patient's prior consent had been secured or if a variety of alternatives had been followed. James Rachels, a professor of philosophy at the University of Alabama at Birmingham, has traced the historical roots of the current debate. He suggests that for a mercy killing, the accused should be able to show as rigorous a defense as would be required in the case of killing in self-defense.[33]

THE SECULAR VISION

The material covered in this and the preceding chapter is intended to document the fact that medical bioethics has been preoccupied with a narrow and constricted view of individual interests that oftentimes does not function in the best interests of either individuals or society. It is also clear that the problems are so overwhelming and the dilemmas so deep-rooted that a reluctance to consider ecological or survival issues may be understood if not excused. A great number of issues in medical bioethics involve a balancing of the individual autonomy of the patient with the needs and desires of his physician, the hospital, and the health care system. Some of the dilemmas might be better resolved if the broader needs of society and future individuals could also be weighed in the balance.

The further evolution of a medical bioethics program has been vigorously promoted by Engelhardt (*Foundations*). After concluding that we inevitably must live in a society of secular and religious pluralism, he expresses the hope that this can be a peaceable evolution.

> In particular, we will need to learn to deliver health
> care in a context of a plurality of moral viewpoints,
> where there is limited moral authority to impose
> one understanding on all without their consent. In
> understanding the limits of reason and [the limits
> of] moral authority to use force, we will come to
> learn much about the human condition. (ix)

Engelhardt presents a "morality of mutual respect"
and demands "a commitment to a secular pluralist
ethic" (385). He offers arguments for abortion on
demand as well as for infanticide and euthanasia
under a variety of circumstances. In so doing he
argues that such views "are intellectually unavoidable even for the most committed Christian, Jew,
Buddhist, or Communist *who does not wish to use
force to resolve moral disputes"* (385, italics added).
(Curiously enough, Islam and the committed
Moslem were neglected throughout the volume.)

Engelhardt does not advocate the abandonment
of the moral traditions of established religion *by
their committed advocates;* what he stresses is that
the advocates must at the same time accept the
propositions of a secular pluralist morality in that
"there is no rational warrant for the use of force in
imposing any one particular view of the good life
on others" (*Foundations,* 385). This defense of the
principle of personal autonomy (85) travels on
rather thin ice even within the health care system
that is the province of medical bioethics, and is
quite different from the concept of "mutual coer-
cion mutually agreed upon" advocated by Garrett
Hardin in his classic essay "The Tragedy of the
Commons."[34] However, the latter view is flawed in
that there is little hope that a pluralist society can
mutually agree to force compliance with a particular
moral view, e.g., absolute prohibition of abortion.
Crowe has emphasized the improbability that
Hardin's theoretical solution can succeed in practice

because all of the needed components are myths that time has seriously eroded: the myth of a common value system, the myth of a mutually agreed upon monopoly of coercive force, and the myth that administrators can regulate the commons.[35] Crowe concluded sadly that the major problems of overpopulation, nuclear war, and environmental degradation have neither technical nor political solutions, while extensions in morality are not likely. His only hope was the enlistment of scientists in the search for solutions. Unfortunately, Engelhardt's excellent survey of where we stand in the philosophic issues involved in health care delivery and the vision of a secular pluralist morality without the application of force did not extend to the essays by Hardin and by Crowe or to Leopold's land ethic. Engelhardt's commendable vision of a peaceful, secular, pluralist society needs to be extended beyond the issues of health care for individuals, beyond the conflicting value differences of traditional religions, and into the biological realities that shaped "The Land Ethic."

---

1. Linda Hughey Holt, "DRGs (Diagnostic Related Groups): The Doctors' Dilemma," *Perspectives in Biology and Medicine* 29 (1986): 219–26. "The bind from a health care-planning point of view is that costs will best be contained by direct disincentive to overutilization of services by physicians, but the moral imperatives of the physician's oath are violated by direct disincentives. Physicians are comfortable either doing everything that can possibly be done for patients or (with) sending the patients to another source of care [sic]; conscientious physicians may find it impossible to function under a system in which they are expected to serve truly as gatekeepers for the rationing of medical care."

2. Joseph B. Kirsner, "The Changing Medical Scene (1929–1985): A Personal Perspective," *Perspectives in Biology and Medicine* 29 (1986): 227–42. Some titles referred to include "Medicine on the Brink: The Dilemma of a Learned Profession"; "The Academic Medical Center: A Stressed American Institution"; "The Young Physician—Living with Uncertainty"; and many others.

3. Clements and Ciccone, "Applied Clinical Ethics or Universal Principles," 121–23. Their point of view is discussed in my chapter 4.

4. Trosko, "Scientific Views of Human Nature," 70–97.

5. Devall and Sessions, *Deep Ecology*.

6. U.S. Congress, House, *A Report of the Select Committee on Children, Youth, and Families,* 99th Cong., 1st sess., 1985, ix. Subsequent statistics are taken from this report.

7. Maureen Hack and Avroy A. Fanaroff, "Changes in the Delivery Room Care of the Extremely Small Infant (<750 g): Effects on Morbidity and Outcome," *New England Journal of Medicine* 314 (1986): 660–64. "Since pessimism prevails in the few reports on *later outcomes* among these very small and immature infants, the *indiscriminate initiation of intensive care* raises many philosophical, ethical, and economic questions [10 references]. Despite many reviews with titles such as "How Small is Too Small," "What is the Lower Limit of Viability?" and "Where and How to Draw the Line," *no clear guidelines* dictate the initial delivery room care of the extremely immature infant (<750 g)" (italics added).

8. Daniel P. Moynihan, *Family and Nation* (New York: Harcourt, Brace, Jovanovich, 1986). Loaded with data and tart, reasonable inferences.

9. Abortion Prevention and Family Responsibility Act, 1985 Wisconsin Act 56, 12 November 1985.

10. Callahan, "Shattuck Lecture." See chapter 4, note 13.

11. R. S. Duff and A. G. M. Campbell, "Moral and Ethical Dilemmas in the Special-Care Nursery," *New England Journal of Medicine* 289 (1973): 890–94.

12. Anthony Shaw, "Dilemmas of 'Informed Consent' in Children," *New England Journal of Medicine* 289 (1973): 885–90.

13. Robert F. Weir, *Selective Nontreatment of Handicapped Newborns. Moral Dilemmas in Neonatal Medicine* (New York: Oxford University Press, 1984).
14. Jeff Lyon, *Playing God in the Nursery* (New York, London: W. W. Norton, 1985). The Baby Doe incident (pp. 21–58) involved a six-pound baby boy born in Bloomington, Indiana, on 9 April 1982 with multiple defects that would require surgical correction and other abnormalities that would remain. The decision was whether to act quickly with considerable uncertainty as to the ultimate outcome or to do nothing (withhold treatment), in which case the baby would surely die. The parents had two healthy children and had looked forward to the birth of a third child. After hearing the possible options from three physicians, the parents chose to have treatment withheld, a decision that was not unanimously approved by the three physicians. Following legal action initiated by the hospital lawyer, a hearing was held and a judge ruled that since medical opinions were divergent, the parents had the right to make the decision. After repeated hearings and appeals all the way to the Indiana Supreme Court, with the media finally alerted and with the special-care nurses protesting the action, Baby Doe finally died six days after his birth. The publicity attending this case, in contrast to the forty-three cases reported in a medical journal (Duff and Campbell, n. 11 above) nine years earlier, set off a series of actions by the Reagan administration in response to further cases and protests by organized citizens' groups.
15. Elliot Slater, "Health Service or Sickness Service," *British Medical Journal* 4 (1971): ;734–36.
16. Richard L. Landau and James M. Gustafson, "Commentary: Death is Not the Enemy," *Journal of the American Medical Association* 252 (1984): 2458. Dr. Landau is editor-in-chief of *Perspectives in Biology and Medicine.*
17. See Weir, "Selective Nontreatment."
18. Stuart Taylor, Jr., "High Court Upsets U.S. Intervention on Infants' Lives," *New York Times* 10 June 1986.
19. Associated Press, "Catholics, Jews Reach Accord on Treating Disabled Infants," *Wisconsin State Journal,* 27 July 1985.

20. Michael Tooley, *Abortion and Infanticide* (New York: Oxford University Press, 1983). See my chapter 7, n. 10.

21. H. Tristram Engelhardt, Jr., *The Foundations of Bioethics* (New York: Oxford University Press, 1986).

22. V. R. Potter, "Applied Bioethics and the Crisis in Health Care," *Psychiatric Annals* 16 (1986): 399–401. The emphasis on responsibilty is in line with "the feminine viewpoint" mentioned in Chapter 4, with Leopold's ideas in general, and with the proposed evolution of a global bioethic (chapter 7).

23. Alan L. Otten, "Wrongful Life? Parents and Newborns Win New Legal Rights to Sue for Malpractice," *Wall Street Journal,* 7 June 1985, 1; Associated Press, Los Angeles, "$2.2 Million Septuplet Suit Filed," *Wisconsin State Journal,* 9 October 1985.

24. H. T. Engelhardt, Jr., "Euthanasia and Children: The Injury of Continued Existence," *Journal of Pediatrics* 83 (1973): 170–71; R. A. Spitz, "Hospitalism: An Inquiry into the Genesis of Psychiatric Conditions in Early Childhood," *Psychoanalytic Study of the Child* 1 (1945): 53–74.

25. It is important to distinguish here between two kinds of brain deficiency. There is a "whole-brain" definition of death in which artificial respiration can maintain a biologically alive set of organs. This legal definition of death began in about 1970. More recently a higher-brain-centers definition of death has been suggested. An individual might not require artificial respiration but remain permanently unconscious (Engelhardt, *Foundations,* 203–16). A newborn infant with anencephaly has a functioning brainstem but no higher brain function.

26. Michael Seiler and Harry Nelson, "Baby Jesse Gets a Heart from Michigan Child," *Los Angeles Times,* 11 June 1986, 1. Jesse Dean Sepulveda was born on May 25 with "hypoplastic left heart syndrome," a fatal defect. A transplant was initially denied on the basis that his unwed seventeen-year-old mother would be unable to provide the needed post-operative care. The Right to Life League of Southern California, an anti-abortion group, and the Pasadena priest who had christened the infant called the attention of the press to the child's plight and the grandparents stepped forward to take

over guardianship. Meanwhile, Frank Edward Clemenshaw, Jr., also born on May 25, was in Butterworth Hospital in Grand Rapids, Michigan, and was diagnosed as brain-dead. With his parents' consent, the Michigan infant was flown to Norton Air Force Base in a private jet-ambulance and transferred to the Loma Linda Medical Center in Loma Linda, California, where he arrived with a strongly beating heart. The transfer was performed on Tuesday night, 10 June 1986, by Dr. Leonard Bailey, who had performed four previous successful transplants since November 1985. Dr. Bailey estimated the cost of the operation at about $100,000, which was borne by the hospital. The operation was declared a success and after some days the child was released to his parents and grandparents. The operation has become possible because the recipients are treated with the anti-rejection drug cyclosporin, administered daily for life at an annual cost of $6,000.

More recently an extensive article has appeared because of the confusion in the definition of brain death (Sandra Blakeslee, "Law Thwarts Effort to Donate Infants' Organs," *New York Times* 9 September 1986, 19–20). Ms. Blakeslee quoted Dr. Michael Harrison, a pediatric surgeon at the University of California, San Francisco, who gave an estimate of 400–500 infants needing new kidneys, 400–500 needing hearts, and 500–1,000 needing livers annually in the United States. A colleague, Dr. Mitchell Golbus, estimated that about 3,500 anencephalic newborns are born in the United States each year, enough to cover the estimated need for organ replacement, but the law has been interpreted to mean that an anencephalic newborn is not brain-dead since it is not whole-brain dead, and the transplant cannot legally be carried out while the brainstem and organs are viable. Pressure to legalize the use of anencephalic newborns for organ transplants is building, while the bioethical ramifications remain controversial.

27. Associated Press, "Organ Transplanting has Non-Medical Problems," *Sious City Journal,* 16 March 1986. (An Editor's Note points out that Dr. Starzl was a native of LeMars, Iowa. He performed the world's first successful liver transplant in 1967 at the University of Colorado.) "From 1981 through 1985 Starzl and other

surgeons at the University of Pittsburgh transplanted 634 livers, 768 kidneys, 198 hearts, 32 heart-lungs, 16 pancreases and three single lungs. Thirty-two times they transplanted a heart and lungs simultaneously, three times a heart and liver. . . . In 1985, 35 other medical centers transplanted livers, 70 centers were transplanting hearts, 180 transplanting kidneys and 20 using pancreases. Most of these began after the drug [cyclosporin] became generally available in 1983."

28. Robert Pear, "Federal Payment for Transplants for Poor Studied," *New York Times,* 18 May 1986, 1. The concept of maximum application of medical high technology has been criticized by an expert on contrasting health care delivery systems (Odin Anderson, "Medical Technology, Ethics and Equity; Current Status and Emerging Issues," *International Journal of Technology Assessment in Health Care,* 1987. He questions the policy of maximum use of organ transplantation techniques and the demand for "presumed consent" by brain-dead donors, and, indeed, what follows: the pressure for voluntary consent.

29. V. R. Potter, "Sequential Blocking of Metabolic Pathways *In Vivo,*" *Proceedings of the Society for Experimental Biology and Medicine* 76 (1951): 41–46. This reference and more recent studies (see L. M. Hall, "Preferential Oxidation of Acetoacetate by the Perfused Heart," *Biochemical and Biophysical Research Communications* 6 [1961]: 177), suggest that in a fasting or exercising animal the liver may export the end products of fat metabolism to support the oxidative metabolism of the heart.

30. P. T. Manning et al., "Vasopressin-Stimulated Release of Atriopeptin: Endocrine Antagonists in Fluid Homeostatis," *Science* 229 (1985): 395.

31. United Press International, "Multiple Strokes Kill 'Bionic Bill' Schroeder," *Milwaukee Sentinel,* 7 August 1986, 1. Mr. Schroeder died on 7 August. He received the implant on 25 November 1984 and suffered strokes on 13 December 1984, May 1985, and on 10 November 1985. He was the last surviving recipient of a permanent implant of a plastic pump, with which he lived 620 days. The temporary use of the device seems to be the direction in which the technology is moving.

32. "Death Out of the Closet," editorial, *New York Times,* 30 June 1986.

33. James Rachels, *The End of Life, Euthanasia and Morality* (New York: Oxford University Press, 1986). In a recent poll of 2,000 people, 90 percent supported the right of competent persons to refuse life-sustaining treatment even if their doctors and their families object (H. A. Schmeck, Jr., *New York Times,* 2 December 1986, 1).

34. Garrett Hardin, "The Tragedy of the Commons." *Science* 162 (1968): 1243-8.

35. Beryl L. Crowe, "The Tragedy of the Commons Revisited," *Science* 166 (1969): 1103–7.

———————— 6 ————————

THE CONTROL OF
HUMAN FERTILITY

ALDO LEOPOLD WAS APPREHENSIVE about a future involving further increases in population in the Western Hemisphere, basing his views on the concept of "carrying capacity" of the land, that is, the soil, water, air, plants, and animals available to the human species. I am sure that were he living today, he would be aware of the precarious future for people in Africa, the Middle East, India, and Southeast Asia.

Today, specialists in a variety of technologies are inclined to believe that if they could be given adequate financial support, there is an almost unlimited extent to which they could expand the carrying capacity of the planet Earth, and therefore the ability to support vast increases in the numbers of human inhabitants in this environment. Their confidence is not justified. No one knows exactly when the point of no return in the present trajectory will be reached, but as Leopold wisely noted, "Ecology knows of no population density relationship that holds for indefinitely wide limits. All gains from

density are subject to a law of diminishing returns"
(*Almanac,* 1987, 220).

In contrast to the cornucopian scenario, there is
another that is much more likely and is in fact
already on stage. It goes somewhat in the following
steps, with one leading to the next.

1. Carrying capacity is increased by technology.
2. Population increases by medical technology and
   environmental technology.
3. Governments and private multi-national corporations are unable to manage ethical problems of
   distribution and equity.
4. Political unrest escalates among competing ethnic and religious groups.
5. Military solutions through exploitation and
   appropriation of science and technology are
   sought.
6. Development of science and technology for the
   common good withers because of competition
   with military demands.
7. Carrying capacity relative to human needs
   begins to enter crash phase.
8. Widespread lowering of lifespan results.
9. Miserable survival remains as the outcome.

Every transition from one step to another in the
above sequence could be the subject of an extended
presentation of facts and opinions, pro and con.
Here they provide a kind of study plan for examining the onrush of daily events reported by the
media.

Aldo Leopold's ethical concern for "the land" is
not only a moral issue but a pragmatic formula for
survival. His views impinge on the very beginnings
of the above scenario. (1) When technology is
employed to increase the short-term carrying capacity of the earth, it must simultaneously be used to
preserve the long-term carrying capacity. (2) When

the population increases as a result of decreases in infant mortality and other preventable diseases, medical technology must also be applied to the goal of controlled fertility.

The present medical pursuit of life maintenance without regard to the quality of life must be carefully scrutinized. While some consideration must be given to the wishes and best interests of those whose lives are pointlessly prolonged, more effort should be devoted to the public health measures that would make possible productive, healthy, functioning lives for people everywhere. It is maintained that this goal cannot be achieved within an ethic that gives top priority to the principle of autonomy, especially insofar as this implies freedom to reproduce without responsibility and without societal restrictions, or within a religious ethic that forbids artificial contraception or abortion.

TWO KINDS OF PEOPLE

Using a system that has profound consequences for the future of the human species, all of the world's people can be classified into just two groups. The separation into two groups can be made on the basis of whether individual couples or single women (including teenagers) are controlling their own fertility, either by means of abstinence, artificial contraception, or abortion. Political problems arise when there is a marked disparity in birthrates among ethnic or religious groups within a nation or between contiguous nations.

In general, the extent of fertility control increases with the amount of education and the breaking away from religious precepts that forbid artificial contraception and abortion. When a city or a nation contains factions that differ widely in their levels of education, income, and religious orientation, political unity may be almost impossible to achieve, and the relative proportions of those with small families to those with large families may change markedly in a few decades. Thus, Norman Berrill concluded (see chapter 2) "that always the more fertile or the more prolific human strains or races will outbreed the rest, that population control by any group sooner or later seals its own doom, with those who retain an uncontrollable breeding instinct taking its place."

There is a tendency in the United States to regard overpopulation as a nonissue, because artificial contraception buttressed by legal abortion is so widespread. (In contrast to the official Vatican position, many Catholics use artificial contraceptives, while those who do not are likely to use the approved natural rhythm method—which is certainly not a "natural" method of birth control.) Yet there is a tragic tendency for the poorest and most disadvantaged members of our society to disregard contraception. The net result can be high rates of teenage pregnancy, increased incidence of AIDS (Acquired Immune Deficiency Syndrome), and a continuation of the poverty cycle for this sector of the population.

The disinterest in the population problem in the United States is sheerest folly for another reason. South of the border, Mexico, with a population of 83.8 million in 1987, has a doubling time estimated at only 28 years.[1] Although Mexico is now making remarkable progress in promoting birth control, the mothers of the future have already been born. With widespread poverty and unemployment it is difficult to prevent unwanted pregnancies. The solution for the disenfranchised is mass migration across the border into the United States by legal or illegal means. Not only Mexicans but Central Americans

from farther south can come in via Mexico. Caribbean populations like those in Haiti, Jamaica, Cuba,
and Puerto Rico tend to fall into this same category
and to regard the United States as a panacea.

For those who, like Aldo Leopold, believe that
"North America has a chance for permanence if she
can contrive to limit her population density," the
control of human fertility is a paramount require-
ment. With a continual influx of legal and illegal
emigrants from the countries south of the border
and from the Caribbean countries and elsewhere, it
becomes apparent that limiting fertility in the
United States, without similar action in other parts
of the world, would not prevent continued
increases in the total population of the North
American continent.[2]

Nowhere are the consequences of fertility control or the lack of it more politically devastating
than in the case of the conflict between the Israeli
Jews and the Palestinian people, although strangely,
the issue has received little publicity. The future of
Israel is fundamentally hopeless insofar as the
Jewish component of the state, which chooses education, science, advanced technology, and a decent
income for its people as its top priorities, operates
within a secular framework that sanctions controlled fertility. Whether the Palestinians are given
citizenship and incorporated into the state or, alter-
natively, are given contiguous territory and allowed
to set up their own state, the demographic balance
will inexorably shift to a situation that will doom
the Jews. Nor can the Jews solve their problem by
an all-out effort to outbreed the Palestinians. It is too
late in their history for that. The Palestinians,
Egyptians, indeed the whole Moslem world—for
whom artificial contraception and abortion are
strictly forbidden—are on a collision course with
the rest of us in terms of birthrates. While

Palestinian women are encouraged to bear five, six, or seven children—to double their group's population in a generation, the Israelis may fail to even maintain their numbers except by immigration. This has further complicated the volatile situation in the Middle East.

Another example of this disparity in birthrates among ethnic groups within a region is in the USSR. Any data on birthrate for the USSR as a whole is meaningless, as in the case of any other country, including the United States, which has widely divergent ethnic groups. Mother Russia and the six Eastern European members of the USSR and its allies are, as a whole, fairly stable in terms of population. In the predominant group, the core Russian Republic, the 1980–81 increase in the population was 0.6 percent, with a doubling time of 121 years. In the Ukraine, Belorussia, Moldavia, Estonia, Latvia, and Lithuania, the corresponding increase ranged from 0.4 to 0.8 percent with doubling times of 93 to 175 years. Numbers of abortions per woman are extremely high.[3] The birthrate is below maintenance levels because sexual activity is consciously moderated very significantly by abortions, owing to a lack of adequate supplies of artificial contraceptives.

In contrast are the Moslem provinces on the southern border where abortion and contraceptives are forbidden. In the four Central Asian Republics of Kirgiziya, Tadzhikistan, Turkmenistan, and Uzbekistan, the 1980–81 increase in the respective populations was 1.8 to 2.7 percent with doubling times of 26 to 39 years. These four republics are overwhelmingly of the Moslem faith. In the Transcaucasus, Armenia and Azerbaydzhan have growth rates of 1.5 percent each with projected doubling times of 48 years.[4] But trouble between the Christian Armenians and the Moslem Azerbaydzhanis has gone on for centuries, and only recently clashes have occurred in Sumgait, a city of 200,000 on the Caspian Sea.[5] Populations of both groups are reproducing much more rapidly than are the core Russians. The Azerbaydzhanis are Shiite Moslems, the sect that holds sway under the Ayatollah Khomeini in Iran where a 1987 population of 50.4 million is reproducing with a doubling time of 21 years (Fornos, *Gaining People*).

Black Africa as a whole has a pronounced population problem. Today a new variable has complicated the picture. With a plague of Biblical proportions threatening, the spreading incidence of AIDS lends a sense of urgency to the need to halt unregulated population growth. According to Werner Fornos, president of the Population Institute, Kenya, with a population of 24 million in 1987, has a growth rate of 4 percent per year and a doubling time of only 16 years. Similarly, Nigeria, Tanzania, and Zaire have doubling times of 23, 20, and 23 years, respectively, some of the most rapid growth rates in the world (Fornos, *Gaining People*). White South Africa, with its controlled fertility rates, undoubtedly feels threatened (politically and otherwise) by these trends. The incidence of AIDS is not unrelated to the unregulated sexual activity in these areas, and perhaps the only break in the rate of increase will occur if the spread of AIDS is unabated.

Leopold was not taking a global view when he proposed the land ethic, nor could he envisage the medical options and ethical dilemmas that would develop over the ensuing fifty years. Today, the issue of controlled human fertility extends far beyond China and India. It is a global problem, and all the values that Leopold held dear will only move inexorably toward ecocatastrophe unless world leaders and their constituents can reach some measure of agreement on how to proceed. Stephen Raushenbush placed the burden of finding a solution in political terms on the United States when he said,

> On the American success in achieving a mutually satisfying way of living, an agreement for common progress with its own minority, which is both underprivileged and racially different, may also depend some of the world's future chances of avoiding centuries of malevolent and violent conflict between the world's dominant white minority and its overwhelming majority of yellow, brown, and black men who are both underprivileged and exasperated."[6]

THE SAN ANTONIO CONNECTION

It seemed entirely appropriate that the Department of Obstetrics and Gynecology at the University of Texas Health Science Center at San Antonio, only a little over a hundred miles from the Rio Grande, would have the vision to see the population problem not only as a North American problem but as a global problem. Under the leadership of Dr. Carl J. Pauerstein, a five-year grant was obtained from the Rockefeller Foundation to set up a post-doctoral program consisting of a six-month core curriculum of didactic instruction in social science, reproductive biology, and clinical procedures, followed by individual specialization in one of these areas. Because of the varying national, ethnic and academic backgrounds of the post-doctoral fellows, the core curriculum was taught with the aid of written instructional units; the outgrowth of that effort was the book *Fertility Control: Biologic and Behavioral Aspects,* edited by Rochelle N. Shain, Ph.D. (anthropology) and Carl J. Pauerstein, MD.[7] For perhaps the first time, the authors reported a multidisciplinary effort combining (1) basic reproductive biology, (2) clinical applications of reproductive and behavioral science (i.e., control of fertility), (3) demography, (4) anthropologic and sociologic perspectives, and (5) social science methodology. Although the disciplines of medical bioethics and ecological bioethics were not included, this omission is readily accounted for by the fact that the post-doctoral fellows were being trained to become skilled in all aspects of fertility regulation, the delivery of contraceptive services, and the problems involved in infertility. The inclusion of items (3–5) was to help "prepare them for the multiple and complex problems that they would face upon their return to their countries of origin." The book remains a monument to the group effort; it is well worth utilizing as an objective coverage of one aspect of the global bioethics that is here advocated—the coupling of medical and ecological bioethics.

CLINICAL APPLICATIONS: INFERTILITY

Shepard noted that approximately 15 percent of couples experience infertility.[8] As a result of widespread fertility control and more liberal attitudes toward the rearing of out-of-wedlock children, fewer infants are available for adoption. Many advances in diagnosis and treatment were described as paralleling advances in the control of fertility.

NONSURGICAL METHODS
OF CONTRACEPTION

"Three factors have revolutionized the attitudes of society toward contraception: (1) the threat of rapidly expanding population, (2) the desire for increased personal freedom, and (3) the development of oral contraceptives."[9] The alternatives to oral contraceptives are all less effective than "the pill"; the so-called rhythm or timed-abstinence method was reported to be much less effective, possibly because of indications "that women have a peak of sexual desire coincident with the preovulatory estrogen peak," making abstinence difficult when most needed (73). But the major complication, according to Shepard, aside from recurrent sexual frustration, may involve an increased risk of abnormal offspring and pregnancy wastage if the method fails. Evidence was cited to indicate that 14 to 32 percent of women per year become pregnant using the rhythm method compared to 1 to 3 percent using oral contraceptives (72). Although more studies are needed to substantiate the risk of abnormal offspring due to fertilization of an ovum more than 48 hours after ovulation, the risk of genetic damage would be an excellent example of the bioethical error in sanctioning an abnormal response to a biologically normal function.

The various methods for sterilization of men or women were discussed by Shepard in another chapter and need not be described here. However, it is relevant to note at this point that Pope John Paul II has taken a strong religious viewpoint on what is clearly a problem in medical bioethics when he declared that artificial contraception and sterilization are "always seriously illicit."[10] Indeed, shortly after the international population conference in Mexico City in August 1984, he repeated traditional church teaching that abstinence from sex during a woman's fertile period was the only method of limiting family size that conformed to divine plan; but he added, "the use of infertile periods for conjugal union can, however, be an abuse if the couple is seeking in this way to avoid children for unworthy reasons."[11]

INNOVATIVE APPROACHES
IN CONTRACEPTIVE RESEARCH

Harper and Sanford reviewed newer methods under consideration.[12] At the time of publication, newer applications of the oral contraceptives were being studied as injectable synthetic progestational agents, and more recently these attempts appear to have come to fruition. In research supported in equal measure by the Ford Foundation, Canada's International Development Research Centre, and the Rockefeller Foundation, a new contraceptive technique with five years protection following a single administration has been reported.[13] The original studies by Drs. Sheldon J. Segal and Horacio B. Croxatto led to

> the development of a new form of reversible contraception, an implant that released a progestrin, levonorgestrel, directly into the bloodstream of women, protecting them from pregnancy for five years. . . .During the next several years, it is expected that hundreds of thousands of women will join almost 10,000 of their sisters in 14 developed and developing countries—the pioneers who participated voluntarily in clinical trials over a nine-year period—in using the implant, which has been named Norplant, (a registered trademark owned by the Population Council).

A similar and parallel development with comparable results is in progress in the laboratories of the Swedish pharmaceutical company Kabi-Vitrum in Stockholm.[14]

The availability of five-year protection from pregnancy after a single administration, with ongoing research on improvements in the technique, would seem to offer the possibility of quieting much of the controversy surrounding the abortion issue. Despite the options, however, the ignorance,

innocence, naivete, religious restrictions, or carelessness of many couples makes pregnancy termination by abortion a second line of defense that will
remain controversial for some time to come.

PREGNANCY TERMINATION

Weinberg has discussed the issues surrounding
abortion as well as the various procedures and their
timing.[15]

In Western society, the major options available
to the woman faced with an undesired pregnancy
are marriage, single-parent rearing, offering the
child for adoption, or pregnancy termination. Each
of these has advantages and drawbacks for the
mother in terms of physical and emotional health
and social acceptability.

Pregnancy termination by abortion is the most
utilized option following an unwanted pregnancy.
Although there are data to indicate that one in four
marriages in the United States occur when the
woman is already pregnant at the time of marriage,
there are also data showing an increased incidence
of separation and divorce in such marriages. Moreover, for most teenagers the marriage "solution" frequently means discontinuation of education and
frustration of life or career goals.

Following the legalization of abortion in 1973,
there were in the United States 1.2 million abortions
in 1976 and 1.3 million in 1977, with an estimated
2.5 million women who desired abortion but for
whom services were not available.

Prior to the legalization of abortion, many
women in the United States were forced to utilize
extralegal practitioners, with maternal sepsis and
mortality frequent sequelae. Death rates from septic
abortion have declined 19 percent annually to the

present rate of only 4 per 10,000 procedures performed in the first trimester and 1.6 per 10,000 in
the second trimester. Both these figures are lower
than those for term delivery in the United States.

Total morbidity, the proportion of patients who
experience injury, disease, or other defined complications as a result of a surgical or medical procedure, is reported as 5.5 percent following first-
trimester abortions. The figure rises to 35.8 percent
for second-trimester procedures. Thus a goal of termination services is to diagnose and terminate pregnancy as soon as possible. Various methods are
available and have become reliable at earlier times
than were previously available.

A variety of procedures for abortion are available, depending on the stage of pregnancy. Current
pharmaceutical research indicates the future possibility of self-administered abortion techniques
employing some kind of a chemical. Among the
new developments is nonsurgical pregnancy termination by means that prevent a fertilized ovum from
receiving the chemical support that it needs to survive. Indeed, it has been proposed that the inges-
tion of the appropriate compound once a month,
without any knowledge of whether fertilization had
taken place, would constitute a method of contraception. Those opposed to abortion argue that the
procedure would constitute an abortion if fertilization had taken place. In the absence of knowledge
one way or the other, they would oppose this
method of fertility control. It is clear that nonsurgical methods of abortion, carried out privately with
the use of specified types of medication, would
make it extremely difficult to prevent women from
terminating pregnancies if they so chose. One
approach to the expression of opposition is the
organized boycott of pharmaceutical companies
that produce the medication, or organized pressure

on the FDA to ban the product. One can foresee the development of small companies specializing in abortifacient chemicals or even black-market distribution.

Weinberg notes that despite legalization, abortion is still opposed by certain religious and socio-economic groups. As a result of this opposition, the Hyde Amendment to the Health, Education and Welfare appropriations bill was passed in 1977, dis-allowing the use of any federal funds in furnishing termination services. A similar amendment was passed in 1978 attached to the Defense Department appropriations bill.

> These amendments deny the poor and military per-sonnel on active duty and their dependents funds previously available for abortion unless the preg-nancy to be terminated threatened the physical health of the mother, as attested to by two physi-cians, or resulted from rape or incest, promptly reported to law enforcement or public health authorities. (Shain and Pauerstein, 122)

Of course, the termination of pregnancy by abortion is an unsatisfactory solution to the prob-lem of unwanted pregnancy. The alternatives are either total abstinence or the use of effective contra-ceptive techniques. Sex education in the schools may provide needed information, but parental guid-ance seems most advisable. The information can be provided "after the fact," and termination services should provide adequate counseling, education, and emotional support before, during, and after the procedure. The provision of contraceptive advice is essential. Two studies demonstrate a 93 percent contraceptive acceptance rate after abortion (Shain and Pauerstein, 118–24).

PLANNED INTERVENTION IN
POPULATION CHANGE

According to Browning and Poston,[16] the three main population variables are fertility, mortality, and migration. "Of the three, governments have put their greatest efforts into the control of mortality. Saving lives is unambiguously positive, and no government has ever avowed other than a policy of mortality reduction" (204). Governments have been reluctant to put their coercive powers to use for population ends, except in such clearcut instances as the effort to control contagious disease. Nowhere is this more evident than with respect to fertility. "Only in the last three decades has the 'population problem' with its Cassandra-like prophecies of impending doom, particularly for the developing countries of the world, led governments to reluctantly acknowledge the effect of population change in the developmental process" (205).

Sources of opposition to family planning programs have been mainly ideological. One author has classified the different sources of opposition in Latin America into three categories, but Browning and Poston regard his analysis as equally applicable to many parts of the Third World. First are the nationalists, who believe their country requires a large and growing population. Conservatives are a separate category, often but not invariably associated with religious groups (e.g., Catholic, Muslim, and fundamentalist sects). The conservative position considers birth control programs to be contrary to natural law (however defined) and yet another step in the weakening of the foundation of society—the family and kinship structure. A third category is the leftists, i.e., doctrinal Marxists, who have argued that in a socialist society the problem of overpopulation simply does not exist. In chapter

17 Poston and Browning presented "Four Case
Studies: Mexico, India, China and the United States"
(Shain and Pauerstein, 215–32). Mexico has been
remarkable for the suddenness with which government policy has shifted toward birth control programs. President Lopez Portillo proclaimed his goal
of reduction of the birth rate from 42 to 25 per 1000
as a target to be reached by 1982. This goal was not
reached, although the crude birth rate was down to
32 by 1984.[17]

FERTILITY-REGULATING METHODS
IN PREINDUSTRIAL SOCIETIES

Shain and Lane have surveyed their subject from
an anthropological as well as a historical viewpoint.[18] They declared

> Birth control has been utilized throughout
> recorded history, and in societies representing all
> levels of socioeconomic development. Birth plan-
> ning is not an invention of modern times, but it is as
> old as mankind. Infanticide and abortion have been
> the most prevalent methods of effective fertility-
> regulation utilized throughout history. (244)

The enumerations of the bizarre and exotic methods for inducing abortion used in various parts of
the world attest to the conclusion by Devereux,[19]
quoted by the authors, that "there is every indica-
tion that abortion is an absolutely universal phenomenon, and that it is impossible even to construct an imaginary social system in which no
woman would ever feel at least impelled to abort"
(245).

SOCIAL & RELIGIOUS CORRELATES
OF FERTILITY

Hoppe has reviewed the extensive literature on the causes of the wide variation in fertility in various parts of the world.[20] The factors include education, urbanism, economic status, minority status, and religious orientation. Without pursuing the reasons for and the historical development of religious opposition to fertility control, and especially the opposition to infanticide and abortion, it was noted that considerable variability exists even within well-defined religious groups. Most empirical research on religion and fertility has dealt with differences between Roman Catholics and other major religious groups. It is less often realized that some other religious groups exhibit fertility rates which in general far exceed those of Catholics, and that despite hierarchial objections to artificial contraception and abortion, many Catholics in the United States and elsewhere are able to limit their fertility.

The highest documented fertility of any religious group is found among the Hutterites, a sect now residing in the western United States and Canada. They believe that birth control is "murder" and will lead to eternal damnation.

> A study of one Hutterite colony revealed that the mean number of children born to women who were between 45 and 54 years of age in 1950 was 10.6 despite the fact that the women married at an average age of more than 20 years . . . The crude birth rate in 1948 was 45.9 per 2000 population. (Hoppe, 267)

The increase in the Hutterite population has little effect on the world population, but the fertility rate of the world's Moslem population is another matter. According to Kirk, "Islam has been a more effective barrier to the diffusion of family planning than Catholicism" (Shain and Pauerstein, 267). The effects of Islamic fertility rates on the future of the USSR and the Middle East may constitute a serious threat to world peace.

SIGNIFICANCE

The foregoing pages have not begun to encapsulate the admirable features of the San Antonio effort, with its twenty-seven chapters, extensive bibliographies and comprehensive glossary, tables and charts, assembled by eighteen contributors. What emerges is the fact that fertility can and will be controlled by an increasingly effective assortment of options, ranging from surgical sterilization to a variety of artificial contraceptives to a developing pharmaceutical approach to nonsurgical abortion. As long as there is a separation of church and state, individuals will be able to limit their fertility and governments will be able to maintain freedom of choice. When church and state become one, as in certain Islamic nations, individual choice may be lost and the increase in total population may have political consequences touched on only indirectly by Shain and Pauerstein.

It is noteworthy that this discussion of *fertility control* has not been one of right or wrong, ethically acceptable or unacceptable. While ethicists and religious groups may debate the rights of the fertilized ovum and the morality of sex without reproduction, the pharmaceutical community will continue to make it easier to avoid both issues. In the long run the new venereal disease Acquired Immunity Deficiency Syndrome (AIDS),[21] not here discussed, may have a greater impact on the mores than do the dogmas.

The subject of fertility control has been intro-
duced at this point and the San Antonio effort highlighted to make it clear that the options are available,
and that they are increasing. The authors were not
describing the ethical dilemmas posed, nor were
they undertaking a discussion of the ecological consequences of a failure to achieve fertility control on
a global scale. On the one hand we have the view of
Aldo Leopold and his realization that population
density must be limited before earth's carrying
capacity is exceeded, and on the other a compelling
presentation of the means and the problems connected with "fertility control." We must now proceed to the development of a viable world view.

Overpopulation is not the world's only problem. Equally important is the overconsumption of
nonrenewable resources by the Western world and
the overconsumption of the so-called renewable
resources of soil and forests by the poverty-stricken,
overpopulated nations of the Third World. Controlled fertility and controlled consumption constitute a double track to acceptable survival for the
future. Inhumane treatment of minorities by majorities or of suppressed majorities by powerful minorities is, of course, not the solution to the need to
control individual reproductive powers. Health,
education, and economic justice will do much to
gain the acceptance of constraints applicable to all.
The prevention of unwanted pregnancies and
unwanted births, along with education that would
provide an understanding of the natural and the
political world, might be sufficient to stabilize
world population and stop environmental
degradation.[22]

1. Werner Fornos, *Gaining People, Losing Ground: A Blueprint for Stabilizing World Population* published for the Population Institute, Washington, D.C. (Ephrata, Penn.: Science Press, 1988).

2. R. D. Lamm and G. Imhoff, *The Immigration Time Bomb. The Fragmenting of America* (New York: Dutton, Truman Talley Books, 1985).

3. U.S. Congress, Joint Hearings Before Subcommittees, "The Political Economy of the Soviet Union," 98th Cong., 1st sess., 26 July and 29 September 1983, 88–162.

4. See Fornos, *Gaining People*.

5. Philip Taubman, "Soviet Reports a Major Oil Center in Azerbaijan is Shaken by Riots," *New York Times*, 1 March 1988, 1.

6. Stephen Raushenbush, *Man's Past: Man's Future, A Humanistic History for Tomorrow* (New York: Delacorte Press, 1969). The author reviews the "failures" of previous power structures—Greek, Roman, Church, Spanish, etc.

7. R. N. Shain and C. J. Pauerstein, eds., *Fertility Control: Biologic and Behavioral Aspects* (Hagerstown, Md.: Harper and Row, 1980). The book has an excellent glossary and index and each chapter has a list of sources and references cited in the text. Permission to reproduce passages was granted by Rochelle N. Shain and Carl J. Pauerstein. *Fertility* is defined in demography as the demonstrated production of children. Numerically it is the number of births per year per 1000 members of the population, also termed CBR, the Crude Birth Rate.

8. Marguerite K. Shepard, "Infertility," in *Fertility Control: Biologic and Behavioral Aspects*, ed. R. N. Shain and C. J. Pauerstein (Hagerstown, Md.: Harper and Row, 1980), 57–70.

9. Marguerite K. Shepard, "Nonsurgical Methods of Contraception," in *Fertility Control: Biologic and Behavioral Aspects*, ed. R. N. Shain and C. J. Pauerstein (Hagerstown, Md.: Harper and Row, 1980), 71–84.

10. *New York Times* and Associated Press, *Wisconsin State Journal,* 27 January 1985, reported that in Caracas, Venezuela, Pope John Paul II issued a strong condemnation of contraception, sterilization, divorce, abortion, and euthanasia.

11. "Pope Warns of Abuse in Natural Birth Control," *Milwaukee Sentinel* wire services from Vatican City, 6 September 1984.

12. Michael J. K. Harper and Barbara A. Sanford, "Innovative Approaches in Contraceptive Research," in *Fertility Control: Biologic and Behavioral Aspects*, ed. R. N. Shain and C. J. Pauerstein (Hagerstown, Md.: Harper and Row, 1980), 85–102.

13. Lynn Landman, "The Makings of a New Contraceptive," *RF, An Occasional Report on the Work of the Rockefeller Foundation* (New York: Rockefeller Foundation, 1985), 9–10.

14. Professor L. Bottiger of Kabi-Vitrum, P.O. Box 30064, S-10425, Stockholm, Sweden, in a letter to the author.

15. Paul Weinberg, "Pregnancy Termination," in *Fertility Control: Biologic and Behavioral Aspects*, ed. R. N. Shain and C. J. Pauerstein (Hagerstown, Md.: Harper and Row, 1980), 118–24.

16. Harvey L. Browning and Dudley L. Poston, Jr., "Planned Intervention in Population Change," in *Fertility Control: Biologic and Behavioral Aspects*, ed. R. N. Shain and C. J. Pauerstein (Hagerstown, Md.: Harper and Row, 1980), 204–14.

17. *1984 World Population Data Sheet* (Washington, D.C.: Population Reference Bureau, Inc.). cf.n.7.

18. R. N. Shain and R. A. Lane, "Population Growth and Regulation from a Cross-Cultural Perspective," in *Fertility Control: Biologic and Behavioral Aspects*, ed. R. N. Shain and C. J. Pauerstein (Hagerstown, Md.: Harper and Row, 1980), 235–50. Rochelle Shain has published an updated review, "A Cross-Cultural History of Abortion," *Clinics in Obstetrics and Gynecology* 13 (1986): 1–17.

19. G. Devereux, "A Typological Study of Abortion in 350 Primitive, Ancient and Preindustrial Societies," in *Abortion in America,* ed. H. Rosen (Boston: Beacon Press, 1967), 97.

20. Sue K. Hoppe, "Social and Social-Psychological Correlates of Fertility," in *Fertility Control: Biologic and Behavioral Aspects*, ed. R. N. Shain and C. J. Pauerstein (Hagerstown, Md.: Harper and Row, 1980), 261–76.

21. R. C. Gallo et al., "Frequent Detection and Isolation of Cytopathic Retroviruses (HTLV-III) from Patients with AIDS and at Risk for AIDS," *Science* 225 (1984): 500–503.

Additional reports with citations of research literature have appeared in other reports by Gallo et al., in *Science* 224 (1984): 497, 503, and 506; and *Science* 228 (1985): 593–95. Also see J. W. Curran et al., "The Epidemiology of AIDS: Current Status and Future Prospects," *Science* 229 (1985): 1352–57. "Community prevention programs . . . should be evaluated according to their ability to prevent . . . infection as well as to influence behavior" (from the Center for Disease Control, Atlanta, Georgia). The overall picture has not changed substantially in more recent years.

22. William Ophuls, *Ecology and the Politics of Scarcity. Prologue to a Political Theory of the Steady State* (San Francisco: W. H. Freeman and Co., 1977). Ophuls does not cover medical bioethics or dilemmas; in fact, he does not index or mention the word *ethics*. Nonetheless he does what he set out to do in an admirable and useful way.

GLOBAL BIOETHICS DEFINED

IT IS SO EASY TO APPLAUD THE DRAMATIC, thousand-mile flight of an anencephalic infant through the rebuilding of its heart into a defective newborn by a skilled surgeon. It is easy to comprehend the one-on-one relationship between a desperately ill patient and a wise physician, the medical bioethic that sees no second choice, that can always choose life as the supreme value above all other values. Not so easy is the problem, How do we prevent famine in Africa? How do we save the Amazonian rain forest? How does South Africa change its present policies and go on to limit the reproduction and meet the rising expectations of its majority black population in terms of education, land, and jobs? How do we incorporate family planning (i.e., controlled fertility) and the concept of person health into an overall program of health care that includes good nutrition, an absence of preventable disease, and a minimal level of infant mortality in our own highly reproductive segments of the population? How do we achieve health without a runaway population increase? How do we prevent the burgeoning human species from destroying the natural environment upon which human life depends? How do we obtain leadership that understands the urgency of developing a global bioethic which, like Leopold's land ethic, "is a limitation on freedom of action in the struggle for existence"?

Engelhardt has remarked that "one has no intellectual problems, no philosophical problems, if one does not worry about giving reasons."[1] It must here be noted that Lester Brown, Director of Worldwatch Institute, and his colleagues have abundantly given the reasons. It is as if the authors have assumed that if the facts can be assembled and the desirability of human species survival can be assumed, the ethics of "what we must do" will follow automatically. And perhaps they are right. The entire output of Worldwatch Institute, from its annual accounts of "the state of the world"[2] to a long list of relevant reports and books, embraces the issues of human survival and the necessities of both fertility control and environmental preservation.[3] As such, Lester Brown has provided a framework for global bioethics under the rubric of a "sustainable society."[4] He, too, would like to give North America—and the world—"a better chance for permanence."

Still, as individuals we need to have a feeling of direction, a sense of personal identity with something above and beyond our own daily life. A bioethic may fulfill that need, if understood to mean a global bioethic, encompassing not just medical bioethics but ecological bioethics as well and having as its core element the twin concepts of "person health" (described below) and Leopold's land ethic.

Global bioethics is proposed as a secular program of evolving a morality that calls for decisions in health care and in the preservation of the natural environment. It is a morality of responsibility. Although described as a secular program it is not to be confused with *secular humanism*.* Global bio-ethics can coexist with secular humanism as long as it can be agreed upon that the natural laws governing the biosphere—indeed, the universe—are not going to change according to the wishes of individuals, governments, or religious preferences.

In the face of the diverse but determined religious bias of major segments of the world population, both at home and abroad, a global bioethic cannot be based on any single religious dogma; and even if there were no other reason, it must be secular: in an evolving legal framework the global bio-ethic must recruit support from all manner of religious groups on the basis of their persuasion that "quality of life" and "quality of the environment" are goals they can support without losing membership in the segregated moral communities that give them courage and hope. These diverse religious factions must be convinced that terrorism, brutality, and war in support of a unique version of religious truth cannot force the acceptance of their particular moral rules by members of other religious or secular groups. They must be persuaded that mutual respect and tolerance for other groups is part of a viable global bioethic. Bioethics remains what it was originally—a system of morality based on biological knowledge and human values, with the

---

*Secular humanism has been condemned on the basis that it places the human species above or in place of the Judaeo-Christian God. It can also be criticized to the extent that it places the human species above or independent of all other species and the natural laws that govern the operation of the biosphere.

human species accepting responsibility for its own survival and for the preservation of the natural environment.

The emphasis on bioethics in the broader sense—as a system of personal morality—has an interesting parallel with Engelhardt's discussion under the heading "Bioethics and the crisis in values." It seems desirable to quote him at length in light of the above remarks:

> Bioethics is an element of a secular culture and the great-grandchild of the Enlightenment. Because the 1980s have been marked in Iran, the United States, and elsewhere by attempts to return to traditional values and the certainties of religious beliefs, one must wonder what this augurs for bioethics in this special secular sense. However, because the world does not appear on the brink of embracing a particular orthodoxy, and if an orthodoxy is not imposed, as say in Iran or the Soviet Union, bioethics will inevitably develop as a secular fabric of rationality in an era of uncertainty. That is, the existence of open peaceable discussion among divergent groups, such as atheists, Catholics, Jews, Protestants, Marxists, heterosexuals and homosexuals, about public policy issues bearing on health care will press unavoidably for a neutral common language. Bioethics is developing as the lingua franca of a world concerned with health care, but not possessing a common ethical viewpoint. (Engelhardt, 5)

HUMAN HEALTH AS THE GLOBAL BIOETHIC

At the outset it must be clear that individual human health for all the world's people and not for just a chosen few must be a high priority for a global bioethic that has as its goal the survival and improvement of the human race. Indeed, health as the basis for the global bioethic is an admirable end in itself. If widely accepted, many other decisions follow more easily. The adoption of a health ethic should be acceptable to all the diverse religious elements, for no nation, tribe, or religious community has ever regarded malnutrition, parasitism, or disease of any kind as a desirable goal. For instance, infant mortality is a measure of the overall health of a community or a nation: a decrease in infant mortality would indicate progress toward better health.[5] Increases in positive health for all members of society would be improvement, in contrast to those technological advances in medicine that postpone mortality at the cost of an increased morbidity and that place sanctity of life ahead of quality of life.

With the emphasis on worldwide health, a large component of global bioethics is medical bioethics, which was shown in chapter 5 to be in a state of crisis.

MEDICAL BIOETHICS IN PERSPECTIVE

Any program of global bioethics must attempt to develop proposals that take a position with respect to the dilemmas mentioned earlier concerning medical bioethics. These proposals should be cognizant of the present state of the environment and of the need to make medical bioethics complement ecological bioethics. The recent book by Engelhardt, a leading medical philosopher, advances forward-looking proposals in medical bioethics under the rubric of *bioethics,*, but excludes any mention of the existence of the *other* kind of bioethics (see chapter 4). Nevertheless, the author does mention contraception, abortion, and infanticide of severely defective newborns and provides hints that a "secular bioethics" would be a step toward what I propose as a global bioethic. For instance, he first states,

"As this volume will show, there will be few serious general secular moral objections to abortion on request." He then goes on to say, "With all its defects, however, a secular bioethics has numerous virtues. It promises the possibility of providing a context for health care that can encompass in toleration health care givers and receivers with diverse moral perspectives" (12). Clearly limited to the roles of health care givers and receivers, the book does not mention problems of overpopulation or of changes in the environment. Nor does it embrace the concept of positive health for populations local or world-wide as a goal for medical bioethics, as is here proposed as a goal for global bioethics. On the other hand, it remains an outstanding work that contains a wealth of background and insight that cannot be attempted here. No writing in the field of medical bioethics can fail to mention it.

In contrast to Engelhardt's publication, which was obviously written for medical bioethicists, George H. Kieffer, a biologist at the University of Illinois, was commissioned by the American Association for the Advancement of Science to write a study guide on contemporary problems. He did just that, as his title *Bioethics, A Textbook of Issues* makes plain. The book was written for students comprising the vast non-specialist audience. Kieffer pointed out in his preface,

> At least two meanings can be given to the term bioethics. In a narrow sense, it applies to those issues confined to medical matters. And in many minds it is this perception that predominates. A broader, more encompassing view includes not only the issues of biomedicine but those of a non-medical nature as well.[6]

From the standpoint of the global bioethics professed here, the medical and nonmedical issues are interwoven to the extent that neither can be discussed to the exclusion of the other, and Kieffer recognizes that fact in his introduction. In addition, he opens with a chapter on "Ethics and Evolutionary Biology" and one on "Ethical Decision-Making," in which he relates to the discipline of philosophy. It is unavoidable to conclude that the two books are essential complements to each other as a background for building the concept of global bioethics, although neither indexes Dobzhansky or Waddington (see introduction).

THE CONCEPT OF PERSON HEALTH

As a biochemist and enzymologist in the field of cancer research, I have been professionally concerned with the concept of health for many years. I am convinced that the ongoing holistic research on physiological adaptation combined with molecular genetics at the reductionist level, is virtually the key to understanding health and disease. I would like to develop a concept of human health that would go beyond vegetative or animal health. I propose to call it *person health,* that is, health that is the property of a responsible, cognitive, sentient person who is active in maintaining or improving his or her own mental and physical condition. In this sense, a newborn infant does not have person health. Its health is the responsibility of its parents. The infant can be said to have health or to be healthy but it does not have person health.

A significant part of the function of physicians, psychologists, philosophers, and basic scientists should be to join in the effort to construct a global bioethic and to instruct, guide, and aid the public in the attainment of person health. The global bioethic presented here is a concept that could provide a model for people—whatever sex or race—to begin to develop responsibility for their own health. This means taking responsibility for limiting the number of children in a family in order to improve the quality of the community in a manageable quality environment. Through family planning at many local levels a combined medical and ecological bioethics could extend to become an expanding global bioethics. With education and guidance from the above-mentioned physicians, psychologists, philosophers, and basic scientists, knowledge could serve as a catalyst and as a powerful antidote against the poisonous effects of greed, ignorance, and unchecked disease in our world today. Finally, healthy adults could then begin to provide their children with the necessary mentorship that is intrinsic to world health and the future of a stable and productive world ecosystem. This is all in contrast to the present system, as noted by Rene Dubos in 1965: "In the United States, the emphasis is on controlling disease rather than on living more wisely. . . . The public health services . . . do little to define, recognize, or measure the healthy state, let alone the hypothetical condition designated 'positive health.'"[7]

My concept of person health is strongly supported by the realization that people can do much to preserve their own health and prevent disease, as summarized by Kieffer under the heading "Personal responsibility for health—An ethical imperative-"(Kieffer, 334–41). He refers to a blueprint issued by the Department of Health, Education and Welfare that seems to respond to Dubos: "Only by preventing disease from occurring, rather than by treating it later, can we hope to achieve any major improvement in the nation's health. . . . Many of today's health problems are caused by a variety of factors *not susceptible to medical solutions or to direct intervention by the health practitioner*"(italics added here).[8] I make the point that only *persons* can take personal responsibility for their own health, and I call attention to Engelhardt's extended and multi-faceted definition of *person*, particularly in his discussion of "person as moral agent" which he terms "being a person in the strict sense."[9] With this view, a fetus or neonate or even a very young child would not be a person "in the strict sense."[10]

WHAT PERSONS SHOULD DO

If health is seen as something people strive for, and if we have accepted widespread health as part of the global bioethic, we can begin to advise people as to what they *should* do for themselves, recognizing that only persons as moral agents, that is, persons in the strict sense, *can* exercise the needed self-discipline to guard and improve their personal health. Persons who accept this responsibility are then in a position to guide the development of their children and adolescents into healthy adulthood. The guidelines thus become a matter of family morality and strength.[11] The following is a general listing of items that only individual persons in the strict sense can be responsible for.

A BIOETHICAL COMMITMENT FOR PERSON & FAMILY HEALTH

1. I will avoid self-administered drug abuse and addiction: this includes alcohol, cigarettes, cocaine and similar illegal drugs, and even legitimate pharmaceuticals.
2. I will give proper attention to diet and exercise.
3. I will avoid sexually transmitted diseases resulting from sexual promiscuity and carelessness. (The current epidemic of AIDS [Acquired Immune Deficiency Syndrome] is only one of the

many known diseases in this category but it is characterized by high mortality and, at present, no treatment; virgins cannot transmit or acquire the disease from another virgin and they will remain disease-free if cohabiting with one another or living monogamously together, assuming both have never engaged in drug abuse and needle-sharing with infected persons.)

4. I will drive carefully and legally.

5. I will avoid action that leads to unintended and unwanted pregnancy resulting from sexual carelessness and failure to use artificial contraceptives.

6. I will avoid exposure to noxious chemicals or unnecessary radiation. (When these are present in trace amounts they may still cause cancer or hereditary diseases at a low probability; individuals cannot always be aware of their presence and can only be alert to warnings from responsible officials.)

7. I will seek competent professional advice and treatment as early as possible when distressing symptoms are not understood; I will seek some form of health insurance while healthy.

8. I will support local and national government officials and private organizations who provide responsible policies and decisions that facilitate the above individual actions by means of education, economic justice, environmental protection, and public health measures.

It may here be recognized that only the citizens in the developed world can begin to approach the freedom and economic resources needed to exercise the options indicated in the above list. Even here in the United States vast numbers of families, many of whom live below the poverty level, cannot begin to make decisions or take action in their own interest among many of the eight categories listed.

In the underdeveloped world actual starvation is not unknown and parasitism exists to an extent unimaginable in the United States. Fertility control is far from adequate and malnutrition does not stifle conception. Global bioethics calls for determined governmental foreign aid plus charitable and culturally sympathetic efforts to bring down infant mortality, malnutrition, and parasitism while simultaneously assisting governments to promote the birth of healthier but fewer children. The challenge of Islam to a global bioethic remains to be examined, however.

THE RESPONSIBILITY OF PERSONS

Infants and children are not in a position to be responsible for any of the eight principles listed above. When we read about moral development in children we realize that the concepts with which they are indoctrinated, if any, fall short of most of my proposals for individual responsibility.

The case of the adolescent is of prime importance in considering the above remarks on "What Persons Should Do" and on "The Responsibility of Persons." Whether one examines the stages of moral development as seen in boys and men[12] or in girls and women, as studied by Gilligan,[13] there does not seem to be any mention of the rigors of responsibility for health, either for self or for others. Until now, most adolescent boys have been concerned with the development of individuation and autonomy while girls have been primarily concerned with caring, relationships, and responsibility to others (at the expense of individuation and autonomy). The new paradigm of global bioethics, embracing a morality emphasized by Gilligan (see chapter 4), insists that now adolescent boys should learn responsibility as well, while adolescent girls should move toward achieving more personal autonomy and individuation. (This is in contrast to the conception of morality as fairness, in which moral development is tied to the understanding of rights and rules.)

Such a step for adolescents would lead, in an expansive sense, toward a movement of cultural evolution and personal adaptation which would begin to set a better structure and ethical foundation for a worldwide bioethics, wherein people could achieve an individuation and autonomy which would no longer be propped up by sex stereotypes and discrimination. This could lead eventually to a global bioethic extending beyond the current parochialism that would support world health and a reasonable population ethic based on personal integrity, responsibility, concern, and action.

Since a measure of personhood is the ability to take responsibility for one's own health, including the ability to control one's own sexual and reproductive activities rather than following one's biological instincts, it follows that moral development in adolescents under ideal conditions is a process of reaching personhood. For this process to succeed there must be adequate resources, opportunities, and motivation. Thus, in addition to caring for their own health, people who have attained true personhood have the responsibility of helping others, particularly their own offspring, to gain the same status. Personhood is thereby a steppingstone to parenthood, in the best sense. Since the human species is no longer in a position to operate on the basis of instinct alone, it is important for developing adolescents to receive an education that establishes the meaning of person health and the responsibilities they owe to their future offspring. It must be obvious that only a rather small percentage of adults can be said to have achieved success in meeting the aforementioned standards indicated in the "Bioethical Commitment for Person and Family Health." Many manage to avoid any kind of drug abuse or sexually transmitted diseases but fail in varying degrees in the case of the other categories. When it comes to the adolescent years, the list seems almost a litany of what large numbers of them are *not* concerned about. This is more than the customary complaint of the older generation; the pace of cultural change has indeed accelerated, with responsible parenthood facing obstacles unimagined in former years. The value system has neglected the concept of person health and a new look at medical bioethics is called for.

TEENAGE PREGNANCY

This dilemma was presented in chapter 5. Stated "in starkest terms," it was "whether to promote or forbid abortions for [pregnant] teenagers," and a case-by-case approach was called for. Certain criteria should be looked for in each case. The goal should be to prevent all unintended or unwanted pregnancies—indeed, *all* pregnancies in economically insecure and intellectually immature adolescent females. With pregnancy prevented, abortion would not be an issue. In contrast, the community's responsibilities for the welfare and the future life of the *pregnant female* should be given priority over any assumed rights of the fetus. Is the girl capable of accepting personal and parental responsibilities? Was the pregnancy unintended and unwanted? Was it the result of ignorance, carelessness, or rape? Were alcohol, cigarettes, or illegal drugs used during the first trimester of pregnancy? Is the case still in the first trimester? If undesirable chemicals were present, what about the positive likelihood for the production of a premature, underweight, and handicapped infant? Should such an infant be offered to unsuspecting or to knowledgeable couples looking for an opportunity to adopt a newborn? What resources, parental or welfare, are available? Is the involved male known? Is the male in a position to accept responsibility? Is the pregnant female likely to produce a normal infant and to nurture it through a successful adolescence? Will her own adolescence coupled with motherhood lead to competent and morally responsible adulthood? Bioethics calls for decisions based on answers to these questions.

At the outset it must be said that, regardless of the answers to any of the above questions, the pregnant teenage girl who was not ignorant or careless, who was fully aware of what she was doing, and who fully accepted the idea of competent, self-supporting motherhood even as a single parent, should not be coerced or forcefully persuaded to have an abortion. If the pregnancy was intended and wanted she must have been aware of the possibility of abortion and have rejected the idea. But pregnancy as an entry to welfare support should not qualify for parenthood: counseling for and against abortion should be available and the seriousness of parenthood should be discussed. In contrast to rational pregnancy, the young girl aged 13 to 16, ignorant of effective contraception, ignorant of the responsibilities of personal health and of parenthood and possessing no employable skills, should be made aware of the possibility of abortion and should be helped in every way to have a legal, medically competent, and cost-free abortion. The idea that abortion is murder is totally rejected by global bioethics, in my view, while emphasis is placed on the development of person health in the unfortunate victim of society's pressures and her own uncontrolled sexual drive. For girls in the 17–19 age

group and for older women, the same considerations apply. The social system and the local community should pursue the further evolution of bioethics, emphasizing that females should not give
birth unless the pregnancy was planned and wanted
and until the female is ready for competent parenthood for a limited number of children, hopefully
with the help of a competent and willing male. The
issue of timing is most important. Abortions should
be performed in the first trimester. School and
parental instruction should provide knowledge as to
the means and moral choices involved in artificial
contraception, bearing in mind the precepts of
"person health," as well as to diagnostic signs and
probability estimates of pregnancy. With proper
instruction, unwanted pregnancies need not occur.
Thus abortions should not be needed but certainly,
if needed, should not be called for after the first trimester. With new methods of abortion and contraception on the horizon, the possibility of self-
administered, completely private abortions may be
very near.[14]

SELECTIVE NON-TREATMENT OF HANDICAPPED NEWBORNS

The subject and possible responses on this issue
have been exhaustively discussed by Weir and by
Lyons as reported in chapter 5, while the philosophical issues have been discussed by Engelhardt and by
Tooley,[15] besides being mentioned above. As in the
case of the abortion issue, killing the result of an
unwanted pregnancy should not be considered murder according to most of the secular philosophers,
although it is not always clear whether their arguments apply to *normal* unwanted newborns. The
present discussion is limited to the dilemma presented by the severely handicapped newborn, and as

before, the matter is one of degree and therefore case-by-case decisions. But again, the proposed global bioethic does not base every decision on the "sanctity of life" model. Decisions must be made on the basis of the type of defect and the ability of medical technology to do more than prolong life. The kind of life in prospect for the newborn, for existing siblings, and for the parents must be considered. Depending on the type of defect, the chances for the birth of a subsequent normal child can be calculated and may be as high as one in four—or higher. If the prospects for development into a self-sufficient person are so bad that the parents cannot accept responsibility for the care and parenting of the defective newborn but must instead have the infant transferred to a public institution, then in consultation with their physician and available specialists they should be permitted legally to make the decision to have the life of the newborn ended in preference to the undesirable aspects of institutional care. Past decisions to withhold care and treatment seem an unsatisfactory alternative to a quick and painless death. (Opposite views are reviewed by Weir.) The maintenance of an anencephalic newborn as an organ bank for a prospective organ-deficient newborn as described in chapter 5 seems more abhorrent than a prompt ending of both newborn lives or, preferably, their abortion as soon as diagnosed. So far it has not been established that the recipients can survive normally (see below). The demand to save the life of every defective fetus or newborn, even though it cannot be given a healthy or tolerable existence, seems inappropriate in the face of the loathesome conditions in which millions of children who are capable of health are forced to live. With no controls on fertility and with the natural environment neglected, the numbers of the deprived will increase while pediatric surgeons seek miracles for a favored few.

Weir has discussed five different alternatives to the dilemma of the defective newborn, along with the polarized positions of the various experts, and personally chooses his fifth, which is to withhold treatment not in the child's best interests. He rightly focuses on the newborn's prospects but, of course, experts will disagree on the child's best interests. In the final analysis the parents, after consultation, should be responsible for the final decision, which should reflect a global bioethic and a consideration for the interests of prior and subsequent offspring.

ORGAN TRANSPLANTATION

In recent years there has been an explosive increase in the number of organ transplants owing to the discovery of the new chemical designated as cyclosporin A, which will permit transplantation of an organ from a donor to a recipient without the necessity of having identical genotypes, as in identical twins, or non-identical but very closely matching genotypes.[16] The risks involved have been discussed,[17] but more recently a new risk has emerged. It appears that cyclosporin A has been shown to act as a tumor promoter in at least one test system.[18] I have previously studied chemical carcinogenesis involving compounds referred to as "promoters."[19] It is now quite clear that certain compounds can, directly or after biological "activation," cause mutations in the DNA of the genome and thereby convert normal cells to "initiated" cells with only a single exposure. It is inferred that most of us have suffered such exposures but that, unless we are exposed over a period of time to conditions that lead to the proliferation of the initiated cell, no cancer will result. Compounds that cause cancer in animals previously exposed to an initiator are called "promoters" and cyclosporin A appears to be such a compound. It is administered daily at considerable expense for the life of the organ recipient. It will be very important to follow the medical history of organ recipients who receive cyclosporin before any conclusions can be drawn as to the possible complications of the cyclosporin regimen. In any case, the rapid increase in organ transplantation is yet another example of the emphasis being given heroic individual health measures while public health measures worldwide inevitably falter. While organ transplantation for defective newborns can be seriously questioned, it can be defended for adults provided the recipient can be given an extension of life with acceptable quality. However, merely to postpone inevitable death at the expense of a miserable life is poor utilization of medical resources.

ARTIFICIAL ORGANS

The tremendous technical advances for adults who have suffered brain damage or loss of limbs in wars and in automobile or industrial accidents will not be discussed except to say that better prevention is still to be preferred. Dialysis machines have been continually improved for kidney patients, and the hope has arisen that a damaged heart can be replaced by a pump of some kind, since the demand for heart transplants far exceeds the supply. Moreover, any decrease in homicides and automobile accidents will further shrink the supply of hearts. Up to the present, patients implanted with a plastic pump have suffered undesirable complications and all have died. It has been suggested that the assumption that the heart can be replaced with a mechanical pump overlooks its metabolic functions.[20]

EUTHANASIA

Nowhere in the whole area of medical bioethics is the emphasis on the postponement of death so pointless as in the case of many of our aged citizens. Residing in nursing homes that are more like warehouses, their only future is greater and greater helplessness until finally the health care system concedes the inevitable. One has only to visit such a facility to realize that its existence as presently conceived is a national embarrassment. Those residents who are not helpless are constantly reminded that they soon will be like those whose company they avoid, unable to command, "Enough."[21] The system is misled by a religiously-inspired ethic that aging or other hopeless humans should not be able to exercise choice in the matter of how or when to die. To the extent that this ethic prevails, it is time for a secular ethic that would permit any individual to ask for help in choosing to die and to make the decision before the ability to make the request is lost. It would be possible to make the loss of the ability to choose between life or death determine when the choice for death is to be exercised. As things now stand, individuals are not allowed to make that choice, and the decision is irrationally delayed until the move to take some terminating action is made by someone else, without authorization by the about-to-die.

As in other dilemmas in medical bioethics, the global bioethic professed here merely demands that we look at the whole picture, that we realize death is not the worst thing that can happen in any individual's life. The ethical issue is not so much the question of whether attention to individual lives is over-emphasized as it is the question of the balance between such efforts and the expenditure of time and money for efforts that would raise the level of personal health worldwide by giving attention to the environment as well as to the technological advances at the medical level.

It is better that one million children should be healthy than that one miserable life should be prolonged against its own persuasion. It is better that we work toward the preservation of a healthy environment than award fame for the creation of the best retrofitted human machine. Thus we come to the ecological reality foreseen by Leopold, that violence to the environment increases with population density.

ECOLOGICAL BIOETHICS IN PERSPECTIVE

Ideally, individuals who are economically secure and intellectually mature should be able to limit their own procreative powers and avoid despoiling the environment. They can even develop their own person health and competently help their limited numbers of offspring to gain personhood. But meanwhile, vast numbers of poverty-stricken, poorly-educated, economically insecure, or intellectually immature females will become pregnant again and again, often beginning as teenagers. Governmental Aid to Families with Dependent Children (AFDC) will have to contribute to their support, while demands for jobs and space continue to exert pressure to mine nonrenewable resources and exploit the environment in a throw-away industrial economy.

There are those who insist that there is no population problem, that the solution will come automatically because of the so-called demographic transition theory of the three-stage shift in the balance between births and deaths. It is claimed on the basis of some past experience that under poor social conditions, high birth rates are balanced by high death rates. As prenatal health care improves, death rates decrease but birth rates remain high and population growth is rapid. In the final stage, fertility—i.e., birth rate—declines and population stabilizes, according to this theory. Lester Brown has provided more coverage of the "whole picture" needed to develop a global bioethic than any other individual or organization. His book, *Building a Sustainable Society,* provides a wealth of data and conclusions. Doubting that Third World nations will move quickly from the second stage to the third stage of population stabilization, he notes that the level of education is a primary factor in lowering fertility. He states,

> Achieving a stationary population will be painfully difficult if contraceptive services are not backed by legal abortion. With the legalization of abortion in Italy in 1978, the share of world population living in societies where abortion is readily available reached two-thirds, up from one-third a decade ago. Yet, one-third of the world's women are still denied this basic public health service except on illicit terms." (Brown, 154–55)

During the Reagan administration in the United States, the view that there is no population problem became official policy and efforts to end or decrease the number of legal abortions at home and abroad were actively pursued.

ETHICS EVOLVES INTO LAW

The conversion of ethical viewpoints into law applies not only to the abortion issue but to every facet of medical and ecological bioethics that enters into a global bioethic. In medical bioethics the legal definition of death has evolved into "brain-dead" but not into "higher-centers brain-dead." The case of assisted suicide can still be interpreted as murder, and letting a newborn defective infant die without treatment is illegal except under very special conditions. However, in some cases an adult may be allowed to die by non-treatment[22] or even with assistance,[23] and for the time being abortion remains legalized.

In medical bioethics the decisions tend to involve a single patient or a newborn infant cared for by a single physician and his consultants, operating in conjunction with the parents, a spouse, or adult children. Still, the decisions operate within existing law. In the case of abortion, individual decisions were revolutionized by the *Roe* v *Wade* decision by the U.S. Supreme Court in 1973, which legalized abortion. Today, attempts are being made by militant groups to overturn that decision and even to write a constitutional amendment making abortion illegal—in other words, to make the law conform to their own particular ethic.

In the conversion of ecological bioethics into law, the scope of the problems becomes much wider. Whether the problem is acid rain abatement or the disposal of toxic waste, governments must deal in general with corporations whose economic interests are at stake. The realization that human ingenuity has created industrial processes and new synthetic chemicals whose benefits find a ready and profitable market, but whose dangers are realized only after hindsight, has created a recapitulation of Pandora's box.[24] All the examples need not be recounted here, but two may be mentioned without extensive documentation.

When tetra-ethyl lead was invented as an anti-knock additive for gasoline used in trucks and motor cars, it was hailed as a triumph of synthetic chemistry and its inventor was congratulated and rewarded. It took nearly half a century for public health authorities to realize that dangerous amounts of lead were entering the environment and for the government to restrict the use of the additive and promote lead-free gasoline. Another famous example is the case of DDT, whose demise was hastened by the publication of one of the most famous exposés of all time, *Silent Spring,* written by Rachel Carson in 1963.[25] Carson has been bitterly criticized on the basis that she described the dangers of this powerful insecticide without mentioning the millions of lives saved by the control of malaria through the cutting down of the mosquito population or any of the other benefits. Hindsight has taught us that DDT, as well as other miracle chemicals such as penicillin, set in motion a present-day proof of the fact of evolution: resistant strains of insects and pathogenic bacteria can evolve and establish themselves in the altered environment, while higher forms of life can be damaged.

Leopold understood this problem when he said, "An ethic may be regarded as a mode of guidance for meeting ecological situations so new or intricate, or involving such deferred reactions, that the path of social expediency is not discernible to the average individual" (see chapter 1). However, Leopold did not foresee the ecological problems that confront us today, problems that the ethics of individual citizens will be unable to cope with except through the conversion of a Leopoldian ethic into law. This process of conversion is a slow and painful development because it seems to require the efforts of private citizens in confrontation with bureaucracy and in a situation where the facts are not completely available. Too often the process evolves after hindsight has revealed the hidden costs in the cost/benefit equation. This hindsight is what Kieffer has referred to as Fontaine's Law: "We believe no evil until the evil is done, if then." He concludes his discussion of ecological bioethics with his initial proposition: "The environmental crisis is an extension of humankind's failure to see itself as an integral part of the global ecosystem" (Kieffer, 376).

Perhaps only hindsight can energize the conversion of a viable global bioethic into law. I propose a generalized sequence of events that may occur as the fruits of hindsight:

1. Environmental damage becomes visible to Leopold's "average individual," raising moral indignation.
2. Knowledlge of these problems evolves a new discipline—ecological bioethics.
3. Moral indignation demands preventive countermeasures.
4. Moral pressure plus factual information generates bioethical guidelines.
5. Guidelines are converted into legal sanctions.[26]

In terms of the polarized positions which accompany the ethical issues of today, the global bioethic would lean toward "quality of life" versus "sanctity of life," and the quality of the environment versus economic growth at all costs ("the sanctity of the dollar"). As currently used, the word sanctity means "assumed to have a value higher than any other value, i.e., second to none." Terms like *quality* and *sanctity* need further explanation and can be justly criticized, unless it is understood that they are here placed on the bargaining table for further discussion by interdisciplinary groups of individuals who have accepted the bioethic of humility, responsibility, and competency.[27] While the control of fertility has been the subject of remarkable technical advances, with still more advances being imminent, possession of the means for fertility control does not automatically solve the problems involved in the search for a global bioethic. Similarly, the problem of how to use ecological knowledge for the social good is confronted with such a complexity of economic special interests that decisions are postponed and avoided.

In a study entitled *Resources and Decisions,* a small interdisciplinary group at the University of Wisconsin proposed that (1) producers of commodities should pay for the identifiable social and environmental costs of production and should pass such costs on to consumers; and (2) public social policies should offer every citizen adequate nutrition, shelter, personal safety, health care, and education. They proclaimed that "there are good reasons to aim for the ideal and there are means available for approaching it."[28] The book is one of the sources of the concept of a global bioethic.

In an attempt to influence society, Jackson, Berry, and Coleman have edited a volume that parallels Lester Brown's *Sustainable Society* in pleading for a "sustainable agriculture."[29] Seventeen highly motivated and idealistic chapters are encapsulated in one sentence in the introduction (xiv), in which Jackson comments, "When the ends merely *justify* the means, there is still time to change, but we are dangerously close to *sanctifying* the means of production agriculture" (xiv, Jackson's italics). My earlier definition, in this chapter, noted that to sanctify would mean to confer a value "higher than any other value, i.e., second to none" and applied it to the idea of "the sanctity of the dollar." But now we come to a consideration of the means, i.e., to the role of technology, which throughout the plea for sustainable agriculture appears as the villain, and with considerable justification.

In an essay that parallels the ideas of Jackson and others, James Trosko uses an analysis of human nature to arrive at implications for the ethics of technological intervention.[30] His thesis is that the values governing the use of technology to gain dominion over the natural environment stem from erroneous views of human nature. These views tend to opt for one or the other extreme of the nature/ nurture argument emphasizing either genetic determination or environmental determination, in contrast to the more scientific view that both play crucial roles.

Possessing a scientific view of human nature (e.g., that human beings are inextricably linked to the biosphere and must conform to the physical laws of the universe), Trosko believes that bioethics is a philosophical alternative to ethical monism and ethical laissez-faire relativism, and he maintains that human values cannot be held in ignorance or in defiance of natural laws. He recognizes that there is no human way that each member of our technological-democratic society can be informed on the plethora of technical and value options. Moreover, he says, such a democracy cannot long survive if it employs a laissez-faire policy in making technological decisions. "To afford technologies the full rights of legal jurisprudence given to human beings in our society will surely lead to major disasters. *In essence, we must now adopt the attitude that technologies are presumed to be guilty until proved innocent*" (91, italics added).

Since we cannot stop the creation of new knowledge and technologies, Trosko thinks it essential to monitor the technological alternatives. "Within bioethics, science and technology can contribute to moral resolutions on three levels: (a) creation of new options; (b) formulating as best it can consequences of these options; and (c) understanding our biological nature and the consequences of the different value choices" (92).

Unfortunately, the fruits of technological advances bear the seeds of disaster in both individual health and environmental preservation. Only an expanded and highly competent core of scientifically and humanistically trained personnel can protect human welfare at the present and at the same time preserve future options. It is inevitable that such efforts will require organization and improvement in the educational system and in the bureaucracy.

The election of political representatives who can face up to the requirements of a new society is failing today because of the conflicting special interests and pressure groups with short-term points of view. What is needed are individuals who understand the dual requirements of a global bioethic and who can band together into organizations like the Sierra Club, the Global Tomorrow Coalition, Population/Environment Balance, and others to publicize and support the election of candidates who have a combination of competence, humility, and responsibility, the necessary ingredients of a global bioethic. At present the environmentalists are fearful of taking a stand on abortion or teenage pregnancy and thus do not name names in the political arena. Yet women could form the backbone of the environmental interest groups, exerting political action both for women's rights and environmental protection. It is also to be hoped that the feminine talent for responsibility and caring could be incorporated into governmental service and corporate management. Cook and Mendelson have gone so far as to suggest that *androgynous management,* combining male and female characteristics, is the key to social responsibility.[31]

What is required is a new breed of political leaders with international breadth of outlook and the sense to call upon informed expertise to examine the options with an outreach toward the future. The idea of "getting the government off our backs" and reducing taxes so that increased material consumption can insure prosperity is a political shell game, epitomized by the Reagan administration. The promotion of person health requires a vast amount of technological expertise to monitor individual communicable diseases (e.g., AIDS), illegal drug consumption, and the protection of our air, water, and food supply, while the improvement of the level of individual knowledge on personal responsibility for person health and parenthood likewise requires organized community input. Similarly, the preservation of environmental integrity requires the monitoring of air and water pollution, the detection of point and nonpoint sources of pollution, and the assessment of plant and animal damage. It is inconceivable that acceptable survival can be guaranteed despite the slashing of appropriations for education, health, environmental protection, and basic research.

Elsewhere I have emphasized that this is not a time for arrogance. I urged a humility in which we admit that not one of us *knows* how society should proceed; a humility that causes us to listen in order to utilize the thoughts of others; and finally, a humility that is not merely a mask for incompetence but rather that is willing to lay its measure of competence on the line, to step over the disciplinary boundary, to criticize and be criticized, and to modify a cherished personal insight through the operation of an interdisciplinary group. Like Leopold, I too believe that "all ethics so far [and yet to be] evolved rest upon a single premise: that the individual is a member of a community of interdependent parts."[32] This global approach to bioethics is urged for the treatment of some of the dilemmas with which we are currently faced.

1. H. Tristram Engelhardt Jr., *The Foundations of Bioethics* (New York: Oxford University Press, 1986), 7. This book discusses the emergence of a secular bioethics if open peaceable discussion among divergent groups develops. Similarly, Pope John Paul II, speaking in Bangladesh to Moslem and Hindu religious leaders and to Protestant and Catholic representatives, expressed the view that political, ideological and economic tensions must be reduced to permit the survival of mankind. While 180,000 Catholics live here, 85 percent of the 103 million people are Moslems. (Associated Press, "Pope Urges Unity for Survival of Man," *Wisconsin State Journal,* 20 November 1986.

2. Lester R. Brown et al., *State of the World 1984. A Worldwatch Institute Report on Progress toward a Sustainable Society* (New York: W. W. Norton, 1984, 1985).

3. A list of the titles of other Norton/Worldwatch books follows in order to give the scope of the Worldwatch effort. In addition to *Building a Sustainable Society* we find:

   a. *The Twenty-Ninth Day: Accommodating Human Needs and Numbers to the Earth's Resources,* by Brown.

   b. *Running on Empty: The Future of the Automobile in an Oil-Short World,* by Brown, Flavin, and Norman.

   c. *Renewable Energy: The Power to Choose,* by Deudney and Flavin.

   d. *Losing Ground: Environmental Stress and World Food Prospects,* by Eckholm.

   e. *The Picture of Health: Environmental Sources of Disease,* by Eckholm.

   f. *Rays of Hope: The Transition to a Post-Petroleum World,* by Hayes.

   g. *The Sisterhood of Man,* by Newland.

   h. *The God That Limps: Science and Technology in the Eighties,* by Norman.

   i. *Helping Ourselves: Local Solutions to Global Problems,* by Stokes.

4. Brown, *Building a Sustainable Society,* 154–55.

5. V. R. Potter, "Can There Be Equity?" in "The Leonardo Scholars," *Resources and Decisions,* ed. Jean M. Lang (North Scituate, Mass.: Duxbury Press, 1975), chap. 10, 142–53. Chapters 1 and 10 were written by Potter with committee suggestions, although authorship of individual chapters was not indicated in the book.

6. George H. Kieffer, *Bioethics, A Textbook of Values* (Reading, Mass.: Addison-Wesley, 1979), iv.

7. Rene Dubos, *Man Adapting* (New Haven: Yale University Press, 1965), 362–63.

8. U.S. Department of Health, Education and Welfare (HEW), *Forward Plan for Health. Fiscal Years 1977–1981,* June 1975.

9. Engelhardt, *Foundations of Bioethics,* 105. "The very notion of a moral community presumes a community of entities that are self-conscious, rational, free to choose, and in possession of a sense of moral concern."

10. Tooley, *Abortion and Infanticide.* See chapter 5, note 20. Written during a stay in the Department of Philosophy in the Research School of Social Sciences of the Australian National University. This author takes up the concept of "person" in great detail, including the scientific evidence pertaining to psychological development and neurophysiological development, as well as the nature of philosophy, which his book seems to illustrate. He discusses the properties of persons, latent persons, potential persons, possible persons, and quasi-persons.

On pages 411–12 he concludes, "There is some reason, then, for thinking that the emergence of at least a limited capacity for thought-episodes may take place at about the age of three months. Therefore, if the property that makes something a person does admit of degrees and is morally significant to whatever degree it is present, there will also be some reason for thinking that humans become quasi-persons at about three months of age.

"The general picture that emerges is as follows. Newborn humans are neither persons nor even quasi-persons, and their destruction is in no way intrinsically wrong. At about the age of three months, however, they probably acquire properties that are morally significant, and that make it to some extent intrinsically wrong to destroy them." From this position, he concludes on page 419, "If the line of thought pursued above is correct, neither abortion, nor infanticide, at least during the first few weeks after birth, is morally wrong." In terms of the U.S. Declaration of Independence, one wonders if all persons are created quasi-equal.

The views of Michael Tooley are placed in context by Robert F. Weir, *Selective Non-Treatment of Handicapped Newborns*. Professor of religious studies at Oklahoma State University, Weir discusses Michael Tooley's position in some detail at seven points in his text. He shows clearly in chapter 6, "Options Among Ethicists" (143–87), that Tooley is at one end of a spectrum that has Paul Ramsey at the opposite end, with other ethicists at all intermediate positions.

He quotes Mary Anne Warren, a professor of philosophy at San Francisco State University, as having views near Tooley's end of the spectrum. She bases the concept of personhood on the following traits: consciousness, reasoning ability, self-motivated activity, the capacity to communicate, and the presence of self-awareness (156).

11. It has been said that humans are the only animals that lack instincts to tell them exactly what to do in any given situation. This idea is only partly true. It is true for humans today because they are no longer in an environment in which they evolved and because they live in cultures that give them mixed messages on "what they should do." Animals in their natural environment have instincts that tell them what to do, but they can be misled in an altered environment. The least that a global bioethic might do would be to tell individuals what to do to be healthy, and to tell society how to help individuals achieve health.

12. L. Kohlberg, *The Philosophy of Moral Development* (San Francisco: Harper and Row, 1981).

13. Gilligan, *In a Different Voice*, 19. Male-centered theories of child development and the contributions of Kohlberg and of Gilligan are covered in a comprehensive textbook by Helen Bee, *The Developing Child*, 4th ed (New York: Harper and Row, 1985).

14. B. Couzinet, N. LeStrat et al. "Termination of Early Pregnancy by the Progesterone Antagonist RU 486

(Mifepristone)," *New England Journal of Medicine* 315 (1986): 1565–70. The compound was given orally in from 2 to 4 days with success in 85 out of 100 women 19 to 42 years of age.

15. See notes 9 and 10 above.

16. P. J. Morris, "Cyclosporin A," *Transplantation* 38 (1981): 349–54.

17. S. Britton and R. Palacios, "Cyclosporin A: Usefulness, Risks, and Mechanisms of Action," *Immunology Review* 65 (1982): 5–22.

18. H. Shinozuka et al., "Enhancement of the Induction of Murine Thymic Lymphomas by Cyclosporin," *Transplantation* 42 (1986): 377–80.

19. V. R. Potter, "Initiation and Promotion in Cancer Formation: The Importance of Studies on Intercellular Communication," *Yale Journal of Biology and Medicine* 53 (1980): 367–84.

20. V. R. Potter, "Letter: Plastic Pumps Do Not Replace Heart Metabolism," *New England Journal of Medicine,* 315 (1986): 1029–30.

21. For aging people who have enjoyed "person health" the increasing sense of the loss of control over their own bodies can actually hasten the decline. Cf. Judith Rodin, "Aging and Health: Effects of the Sense of Control," *Science* 233 (1986): 1271–76, with extensive notes and references. The onset of Alzheimer's disease is the ultimate in loss of control.

22. Associated Press, Boston, "Family Wins in Right-to-Die Ruling," *Wisconsin State Journal,* 12 September 1986, National Digest column. The entire item follows:

    "A brain-damaged man who requires artificial feeding may be removed from a hospital and allowed to starve to death, the Massachusetts Supreme Court ruled Thursday.

    "In a 4–3 opinion, the justices granted the request of Patricia Brophy to stop providing food and water to her husband, Paul E. Brophy Sr., 49, a former firefighter in a coma for 3½ years.

    "Before a blood vessel in his brain ruptured in 1983, Brophy often told his family that he would not want to be kept alive artificially."

The course of conversion of ethics to law proceeds not so much by what we write as by the march of events. There is a fine line between the withholding of artificial feeding and the use of a lethal injection.

23. Derek Humphrey and Ann Wickett, *The Right to Die. Understanding Euthanasia* (New York: Harper and Row, 1986).

24. V. R. Potter, "Dangerous Knowledge: The Dilemma of Modern Science," in *Bioethics,* 70.

25. Rachel Carson, *Silent Spring* (Boston: Houghton Mifflin, 1962). See Paul Brooks, *Speaking for Nature: How Literary Naturalists from Henry Thoreau to Rachel Carson Have Shaped America* (Boston: Houghton Mifflin, 1980). Includes a chapter on Aldo Leopold.

26. V. R. Potter, "Evolving Ethical Concepts," *BioScience* 28 (1977): 251–53.

27. V. R. Potter, "Humility with Responsibility: The First Rule of Professional Ethics," in *The Role of Ethics in American Life,* ed. Robert Preston (Louisville: The Bellarmine College Press, 1977). See also V. R. Potter, "Humility with Responsibility, The Basic Bioethic," *Cancer Research* 35 (1975): 2297–2306; and Potter, "Evolving Ethical Concepts."

28. V. R. Potter, *Resources and Decisions,* xiii. A key distinction between *public goods* (mass transportation, parks, museums, schools, music, literature, experimental research) and *private goods* (automobiles, clothes, small boats, snowmobiles, appliances) was emphasized in chapter 10, "Can There Be Equity," by the present writer, drawing heavily on Carl H. Madden, *Clash of Cultures: Management in an Age of Changing Values* (Washington, D.C.: National Planning Association, 1972).

29. W. Jackson, W. Berry, and B. Coleman, *Meeting the Expectations of the Land. Essays in Sustainable Agriculture and Stewardship* (San Francisco: North Point Press, 1984). See also T. Edens, C. Fridgen, and S. Battenfield, *Sustainable Agriculture* (East Lansing: Michigan State University Press, 1985).

30. James E. Trosko, "Scientific Views of Human Nature: Implications for the Ethics of Technological Intervention," in *The Culture of Biomedicine*, vol. 1, *Studies in Science and Culture,*, ed. D. H. Brock (Cranbury, N.J.: Association of University Presses, 1984), 70–97.

31. S. H. Cook and J. L. Mendelson, "Androgynous Management: Key to Social Responsibility," *Advanced Management Journal* 42 (1977): 25–35.

32. Leopold, *Almanac,* 1987 ed., 203. See chapter 1, note 1.

Appendix 1

THE LEOPOLD
HERITAGE

ALDO LEOPOLD was born on January 11, 1887, in Burlington, Iowa, where his father and grandfathers were prominent citizens. He did graduate work and obtained a master's degree in forestry at the Yale Forest School (where the great conservationist Gifford Pinchot was a professor) in June 1909. He entered the U.S. Forest Service at once and was sent to the new Southwestern District in Arizona and New Mexico. By 1912 Leopold was supervisor of the Carson National Forest in northern New Mexico, "a million acres supporting 200,000 sheep, 7000 head of cattle, 600 homesteads and a billion feet of lumber."[1] In April 1913, in a remote area, he was almost fatally exposed to wet and cold conditions and required eighteen months for recuperation, during which time Flader notes that he may have read the eleven-volume Riverside edition of Thoreau's works, which he had received in 1912 as a wedding gift (Flader, 10).

With the publication in 1933 of his successful

text *Game Management,*[2] Leopold could indulge in "a reorientation in his thinking from a historical and recreational to a predominantly ecological and ethical justification for wilderness" (Flader, 29). In April 1935 Leopold acquired the worn-out, abandoned farm ("the shack") on the Wisconsin River that was to become the setting for most of the nature sketches in *A Sand County Almanac*; here he wrote most of the essays that constitute "The Land Ethic," which, according to Meine,[3] was composed in four phases over a period of fourteen years. This remarkable essay has become the subject of countless articles; indeed, Meine has noted that Leopold was cited in 27 of 96 articles in the first eighteen issues of *Environmental Ethics,* which was founded in 1979.

Quoting Flader, "On April 21, 1948 Aldo Leopold died of a heart attack while helping his neighbors fight a grass fire that threatened his sand-county farm. One week earlier, the book of essays for which he had been seeking a publisher since early 1941 was accepted by Oxford University Press" (35). His son Luna edited the manuscript and saw it through to publication in 1949.

THE LEOPOLD FAMILY HERITAGE

Aldo Leopold was fortunate in his cultural and biological heritage. The record contains abundant material on his German ancestors, all meticulously assembled by Meine in his monumental biography of Leopold.[4] His paternal grandfather, Charles J. J. Leopold, was born in Hanover in 1809, while his maternal grandfather, Charles Starker, was born in 1826 in Stuttgart. Aldo's father, Carl, was born in Burlington, Iowa, in 1858 and grew up with a life-long interest in hunting, which he passed on to his son, along with "something of the family's aristocratic bearing, but without its aristocratic affectations" (8). Carl's parents had continued to receive newspapers from the capitals of Europe.

Aldo's mother, Clara Starker, had traveled with her parents in Europe, where she developed a deep love of grand opera. Years later she made an annual pilgrimage to the opera in Chicago. Clara Starker was Carl Leopold's cousin, inasmuch as their fathers had married sisters (Thusneld Runge Leopold and Marie Runge Starker). Their families were closely intertwined, and German remained the household language until the children enrolled in school.

Meine describes in detail the combination of the love of hunting and the love of nature that Aldo received from his father. At the same time, his mother's influence was to emphasize education and writing. She was responsible for his leaving home to attend the Laurenceville Preparatory School at the age of seventeen. At the same time she began the correspondence between them. Both parents wrote frequently, while Aldo fired off letters "at a rate that sometimes reached four and five letters a week" and that continued until long after Leopold's college days (34). All of these letters were saved and available to Meine, who noted that the letters allowed Leopold to explore and express his absorbing relationship with nature, all the while refining the skills that would one day produce some of the language's most eloquent nature writing. Thus, the combination of a warm and supportive family and perhaps an inborn urge to write provided Leopold with a heritage that sustained him throughout his productive life.

Aldo Leopold was fortunate not only in the heritage he received from his parents, but in the heritage that came to him when he married Estella Bergere. "Her father, Alfred M. Bergere, was among the most prominent men in Santa Fe. Born in Liverpool,

England, to a Franco-Milanese father and a Venetian mother, Bergere had been a musical prodigy, studying piano until he was sixteen, when he left Europe to seek his fortune in America" (110). Ten years later he arrived in the Southwest, "where in 1884 he made the acquaintance of Don Solomon Luna, the leading sheepman and powerbroker in the New Mexico Territory" (110). Bergere married Don Solomon's widowed sister, Eloise Luna Otero. Maria Alvira Estella Bergere was born August 24, 1890, at Los Lunas, New Mexico, the second surviving child in a staunchly Roman Catholic family that grew to include seven sisters, two brothers, two half-brothers, and one half-sister. Because her mother was the sister of Don Solomon Luna, Estella belonged to a family deeply imbedded in the history and lore of the Southwest, Spanish America, Mexico, and Old Spain. The family name, Luna, dated from the year 1091, and Lunas accompanied Cortez and Coronado in the New World. A branch settled between the Rio Grande and the Puerco and eventually acquired 80,000 acres of the San Clemente Grant. As described by Meine, the Luna sheep enterprise was by 1900 said to be the largest in the United States (111). With an abundance of archival letters the courtship of Estella by Aldo could be described in some detail (106–23). The wedding occurred on October 9, 1912, in Santa Fe. Aldo remained a non-Catholic and with some reluctance took a vow not to interfere in the spiritual upbringing of any future children (121–22).

Tragedy struck only six months later in April 1913 when Aldo Leopold developed a case of acute nephritis following several days and nights of exposure to rain and sleet on a horseback field trip made alone (122–23). He spent the sixteen-and-a-half-month period of recuperation, on unpaid leave from the Forest Service, in one or the other parental household. The love and support from both the Leopold and the Bergere families strengthened and tempered the spirits of Aldo and Estella Leopold. Aldo was given time to read, to think, to become a generalist, and to conceive of an entity, "The Forest"—"the timber, water, forage, farm, recreative, game, fish, and aesthetic resources of the areas under our jurisdiction" (126). Clearly, the letter he addressed "to the Forest officers of the Carson," published in 1913, set him on the path toward the larger entity that he was to call "The Land" and to conceive of a still larger concept, "The Land Ethic."

THE LEOPOLD INTELLECTUAL HERITAGE

Roderick Nash has provided a scholarly account not only of Leopold's predecessors but also of his followers up to and including the present author, and traces Leopold's evolving philosophy.[5] Without recapitulating Nash's account, it is worth noting the undoubtedly determinative effort of Leopold's long convalescence in the period between April 23, 1913, and September 14, 1914, during which time he was not even allowed to walk. At one time he was directed to leave the altitude of Santa Fe in favor of the lower altitude of Burlington. In both parental homes he had the decisive influence of enforced leisure which in his case led to much mental activity, supported by the love of family and wife. Aldo Leopold made good use of the time to read and make notes, but the notes were not those of a man who planned to write a book. It was not until about 1941 that he began to think seriously about "a nature book," according to Dennis Ribbens, who traces the correspondence between Leopold and friends and publishers.[6] By that time, all of the reading and writing over a period of over thirty years was not available or necessary for the book Leopold had in mind.

From Curt Meine's book it is evident that much of Aldo Leopold's intellectual heritage came from his family, who provided both nature and nurture. The answer to the mystery of the making of Aldo Leopold can be distilled from Meine's pages. Leopold was pointed in the direction of the land ethic by his parents, but the decisive event was his brush with death and long convalescence.

While the absence of references in the essay on "The Land Ethic" has been noted earlier (see preface), it remained for Nash to comment in detail on the historical roots that Aldo Leopold might have cited and probably was aware of. He remarked, "Whether he acknowledged it or not, Leopold's achievements rested on more than a century of theological, philosophical, and scientific thoughts" (Nash, 64).

---

1. Susan Flader, *Thinking Like a Mountain. Aldo Leopold and the Evolution of an Ecological Attitude Toward Deer, Wolves, and Forests* (Lincoln: University of Nebraska Press, 1978), 9.

2. Aldo Leopold, *Game Management* (New York: Scribners, 1933).

3. Curt Meine, "Building The Land Ethic: A History of Aldo Leopold's Most Important Essay" (M.S. thesis, University of Wisconsin, 1983).

4. Curt Meine, *Aldo Leopold. His Life and Work* (Madison: University of Wisconsin Press, 1988). Includes 529 pages of text and photographs plus 105 pages of bibliographies, notes, and index. Although Flader has been used as a source of some biographical detail in this section, the reader will find much more of interest in Curt Meine's epic book.

5. Roderick Nash, "Aldo Leopold's Intellectual Heritage," in *Companion to A Sand County Almanac. Interpretive and Critical Essays,* ed. J. Baird Callicott (Madison: University of Wisconsin Press, 1987), 63–88.

6. Dennis Ribbens, "The Making of *A Sand County Almanac,*" in *Companion to A Sand County Almanac. Interpretive and Critical Essays,* ed. J. Baird Callicott (Madison: University of Wisconsin Press, 1987), 91–109.

Appendix 2

A BIOETHICAL CREED
FOR INDIVIDUALS

1. **Belief:**
I accept the need for prompt remedial action in a world beset with environmental and religious crises.

Commitment:
I will work with others to improve the formulation of my beliefs, to evolve additional credos, and to seek a worldwide movement that will make possible the survival and improved development of the human species in harmony with the natural environment and with fellow humans.

2. **Belief:**
I accept the fact that the future survival and development of humankind, both culturally and biologically, is strongly conditioned by present activities and plans that affect the biotic environment.

Commitment:
I will try to adopt a life-style and to influence the life-style of others so as to promote the evolution of a better world for future generations of the human species, and I will try to avoid actions that would jeopardize their future by ignoring the role of the natural environment in food and fiber production.

3. Belief:

I accept the uniqueness of each individual and his or her instinctive need to contribute to the betterment of some larger unit of society in a way that is compatible with the long-range needs of society.

Commitment:

I will try to listen to the reasoned viewpoint of others whether from a minority or a majority, and I will recognize the role of emotional commitment in producing effective action.

4. Belief:

I accept the inevitability of some human suffering that must result from the natural disorder in biological creatures and in the physical world, but I do not passively accept the suffering that results from inhumane treatment of individual persons or groups.

Commitment:

I will try to face my own problems with dignity and courage, I will try to assist others when they are afflicted, and I will work toward the goal of eliminating needless suffering among humankind as a whole.

5. Belief:

I accept the finality of death as a necessary part of life. I affirm my veneration for life, my belief in the need for brotherhood now, and my belief that I have an obligation to future generations of the human species.

Commitment:

I will try to live in a way that will benefit the lives of my fellow humans now and in time to come and that will be remembered favorably by those who survive me.

6. Belief:

I believe that society will collapse if the ecosystem becomes irreparably damaged and unless human fertility is brought under worldwide control, given the concomitant increase in the competence of its members for understanding and maintaining human health.

Commitment:

I will try to master a skill or a professional talent that will contribute to the survival and improvement of society and to the maintenance of a healthy ecosystem. I will try to assist others in the development of their potential talents while at the same time maintaining my sense of self-caring, self-esteem, and individual worth.

7. *Belief:*

I believe that each adult person has a personal responsibility for his or her own health as well as a responsibility for the development of this aspect of personhood in any offspring that may be produced.

Commitment:

I will endeavor to carry out the eight obligations described as a Bioethical Commitment for Person and Family Health. I will limit my own reproductive powers in accordance with national and international goals.

INDEX

A

Abortion, 101–4, 140–42, 144, 164–65, 180n.10; data on, 101–2, 140–41; legalization of, 171, 172; non-surgical, 141, 181n.14; and population control, 134; and pro-choice, 97

Abortion Prevention and Family Responsibility Act of 1985, 104

Acid rain, 65–66

Adaptation: cultural, 6–7; evolutionary, 6, 173; physiological, 5, 6, 11n.8, 64, 157. *See also* Evolution

AIDS, 135, 159–60

Almeder, Robert F., 91n.4

Alvarez, W., 54n.15

American Cancer Society, 50

American Jewish Congress, 109

Anderson, Odin, 126n.28

Androgynous Management, 177

Anencephalic newborns. *See* Brain death

Anglemeyer, Mary, xvi n.4

Artificial heart, 118, 126n.31

Artificial organs, 168

B

Baden, John, 66, 70n.11

Battelle Human Affairs Research Centers, 116

Beauchamp, Tom L., 73

Bee, Helen, 181n.13

Bennett, William, 79

Berrill, Norman J., 31, 33–34

Berry, W., 183n.29

Bhopal, India, 49

Biocybernetic systems, 5

Bioethical Commitment for Person and Family Health, 159–60